Reflections in the Land of Jesus

Albert Mosedale

New Wine Press

New Wine Press
PO Box 17
Chichester PO20 6YB
England

ISBN: 1 874367 84 1

Typeset by CRB Associates, Reepham, Norfolk
Printed in England by Clays Ltd, St Ives plc

Dedication

*I lovingly dedicate this book to my dear wife June
in this our Golden Wedding Year.
So much of my ministry has been the result of her faithful
support and encouragement and I honour her for truly being a
wonderful inspiration and companion.*

Contents

Foreword

I first visited Israel with my wife in 1978. That first day spent visiting the Old City of Jerusalem was a unique and life-changing experience. I was spiritually and emotionally bowled over, felt as if I had 'come home', and spent the intervening three years before our next visit with an intense feeling of home sickness, just longing to be back in Jerusalem.

Since then I have visited the land 50 times, which has included leading some 15 tours, mostly with an in-depth study theme, exploring every corner of the land. Even so there is always something fresh to see, some corner not touched. There are many levels of interaction, from the enjoyment of landscape, sea, desert and flowers – and not forgetting felafel – to the depths of the historical and biblical roots of Judaism and Christianity, as well as seeing the remarkable fulfilment of biblical prophecy.

Israel is the ultimate visual aid to understanding the Bible and its message, the land in which God revealed Himself through sages and prophets, and the land in which Jesus lived and taught. Every Christian should go at least once if at all possible.

Albert Mosedale has provided a wonderful travel companion to Israel. He touches on virtually all the places and sites the first, second and even third timer should visit (although no one book can deal with **every** place in this remarkable land). Most important, he infuses his descriptions and teaching with a warm devotional focus which can only bless the reader.

It should be remembered that Christianity grew out of first century Judaism and draws still from the richness of that heritage. The outlines on the *Feasts of the Lord* will help many to rediscover this fact.

I warmly commend *Reflections in the Land of Jesus* to all those preparing to visit Israel, as well as to those who having been already want a companion to help them focus and cement their recollections and explore the devotional aspects of their experience. And for those who cannot (yet) go, it will prove a helpful and heart-warming substitute. May it also encourage prayer for this land and people which is so central to God's purposes in these days.

Derek C. White
Director – Christian Friends of Israel UK

Introduction

With the experience of visiting Israel regularly for more than 20 years and the privilege of introducing many groups and individuals to this Special Land, *Reflections in the Land of Jesus* is compiled in answer to requests that some of the ministry shared might be produced in written form. The book consists of four parts.

Part I does not aim to be a comprehensive travel guide of the Holy Land; there are many excellent publications that already fulfil that function. Rather, it aims to be a 'travel companion' that gives some background information on the chief places that can be visited as well as some others you may have time to see.

In addition, some devotional thoughts and poems have been included that may help keep the memory fresh and perhaps bring some portion of God's Word alive in a new way.

Also, it is hoped that the information contained in Parts II and III will help answer some of those questions that often come to mind when no-one is around to do so!

Part IV is devoted to discussing in some detail the Feasts of the Lord as the author believes it is important to understand how they fit into God's plan of salvation. He has previously shared some of this teaching with a number of church congregations as well as at two conferences arranged by the Messianic Jewish Association of Great Britain.

> 'If we should meet and you forget me,
> you have lost nothing;
> But if you meet **Jesus Christ**
> and forget Him –
> you have lost everything!'

Jesus

Jesus is the image of the God we cannot see,
The first-born out of all the Lord's creation;
For by Jesus God created the heaven, earth and sea,
And all mankind of every generation.
All things hold together by the power of His Word,
In Him all things consist and keep their order.
Allowing man to exercise the free-will he was given,
Brought sin and death – and to the world disorder.
Yet way back in eternity God knew what man would do,
He knew mankind would drown in degradation;
So this great powerful Jesus stepped into history
To establish God's divine plan of salvation.
It had to be the Cross for Him! There was no other way
To bring about that reconciliation
Of bringing us to God, but stripped of every taint of sin,
Ensuring we'd receive Justification!
A standing that is right with God –
as if we'd never sinned!
What glorious grace and love beyond all measure;
Clothed in His righteousness,
appearing in God's holy sight
A purchased people – God's own special treasure!

(Colossians 1:15–16 and Hebrews 1:1–3)

PART I

Places to Visit

For the Lord your God is bringing you into a good land – a land with streams and pools of water, with springs flowing in the valleys and hills; a land with wheat and barley, vines and fig trees, pomegranates, olive oil and honey... (Deuteronomy 8:7, 8)

Introducing Jerusalem

The journey from Ben Gurion airport to Jerusalem is just under 40 miles and will always evoke excitement, especially for the first-time visitor. Whether undertaken by day or night it becomes obvious that the journey is a continuous climb until the City is reached some 2400 feet above sea level.

> *I rejoiced with those who said to me,*
> *'Let us go to the house of the Lord.'*
> *Our feet are standing*
> *in your gates, O Jerusalem.*
> *Jerusalem is built like a city*
> *that is closely compacted together.*
> *That is where the tribes go up,*
> *the tribes of the Lord,*
> *to praise the name of the Lord*
> *according to the statute given to Israel.*
> *There the thrones for judgement stand,*
> *the thrones of the house of David.*
> *Pray for the peace of Jerusalem:*
> *'May those who love you be secure.*
> *May there be peace within your walls*
> *and security within your citadels.'*
> *For the sake of my brothers and friends,*
> *I will say, 'Peace be within you.'*
> *For the sake of the house of the Lord our God,*
> *I will seek your prosperity.*   (Psalm 122)

Established on a number of hills, Jerusalem has existed for 4000 years having been destroyed and rebuilt many times. Grander and vaster cities have been erected and have flourished during that time but none have lasted the course as Jerusalem has. Its name means 'City of Peace', yet its long history is a continuous tale of fighting. When the people were obedient to God they enjoyed victory and blessing but when they embraced the worship of pagan gods they suffered defeat and humiliation at the hands of their enemies.

An excellent introduction to Jerusalem is a morning visit near to the top of the Mount of Olives which lies to the east of the City. The rising sun brings to life a grand panoramic view dominated by the magnificent Dome of the Rock built on the site of the old Jewish Temple and possibly the place of sacrifice where Abraham was tested of God concerning Isaac the son of promise (Genesis 22).

Originally completed by the Caliph Abdel Melek in AD 691 the Dome of the Rock was transformed into a Christian shrine by the Crusaders in 1099 but 90 years later was re-captured by Saladin and completely restored, becoming Islam's holiest site after Mecca and Medina.

A vast restoration programme carried out in 1993/4 was funded with a 10 million dollar gift from Jordan's King Hussein. The dome of anodized aluminum was replaced by a brass coated one with 100 kilos of 24-carat gold valued around $1\frac{1}{2}$ million dollars! It reflects the rays of the morning sun in a blaze of glory; yet how vaster and more wonderful was the Temple of Jesus' day with its shining marble walls and rich gold embellishments!

Greatly extended and lavishly refurbished by Herod the Great from 19 BC the work was still in progress during the lifetime of Jesus and continued until AD 63. Seven years later however it lay in ruins as did the vast majority of the City, as a result of the devastation wrought by the invading Romans under General Titus.

Jerusalem, God's City, your name proclaims God's
    Peace;
Yet ringed with anger, hatred; your tension doesn't
    cease;
Amazing is this paradox! How can a peace exist
With never-ending opposition heading up the list?

Yet God has said this place He makes His special
   habitation,
The City and the Land is His; the Jews His chosen
   Nation.
His Man of Peace is Jesus, and He alone can do
The work of reconciling a God and folk like you;
For Peace means making unity, of blending into one
That which was torn asunder – caused by the Evil
   One.
In Jesus we can find true Peace! Be confident, and
   come
To Father God! united by His own dear precious Son.

The Western Wall

Known the world over and sometimes called the 'Wailing
Wall', this is Jerusalem's main meeting place regarded by
the majority of Jews as specially holy. It is the only visible
reminder they have of their destroyed Temple marking its
western boundary. Strictly speaking, it is not the wall of the
Temple but the retaining wall built by Herod when he
levelled and greatly extended the area surrounding it.

In 1967 when Israel overran the forces of Jordan, the
Wall was the first place the soldiers made for. In those days
the area in front of it was covered with many dwellings
making access extremely cramped and difficult. Today,
with the area cleared and paved, a large attractive plaza
has been created where vast crowds can gather for social or
public occasions.

Sometimes a bride and groom will drive into the square to
be photographed against the backdrop of the Wall; members
of Israel's Paratroopers hold Passing-Out Ceremonies here.
Perhaps one of the most moving gatherings in recent years
occurred on 8 October 1987.

In Deuteronomy 31:10ff we read that the Law was to be
read to all the people every seven years at the Feast of
Tabernacles. This was done in 1987 for the first time since

AD 70! 35,000 crammed the area in front of the Wall as the President read from God's Word, an observance that tied in with the required Sabbatical year as well as Israel's 40th Anniversary.

Directly in front of the Wall men and women come to pray in their own designated sections; thirteen-year old boys celebrate their Bar-mitzvah, and Sabbath groups gather round the Torah (the first five books of the Bible) engaging in serious discussion.

A number of years ago a distraught mother was praying by the Wall beside the barrier that separates the women from the men. Some time previously her teenage son had started to mix with unsavoury company until, addicted to alcohol and drugs he had left home.

People who pray at the Wall will often write a prayer on a piece of paper which they will push into a crack between the stones. As the mother finished praying, such a piece of paper fluttered down from the men's section and fell at her feet. Unfolding it she read a cry for help from someone 'at the end of his tether'. The woman could hardly believe her eyes – it bore her son's name with an address! Hurrying there they were reconciled and he returned home – a real-life enactment of the Prodigal Son. How God loves to answer prayer!

Mea She'arim

The name implies 'a hundredfold' and the Quarter is a stronghold of the Ultra-Orthodox Jews. Established around 1875 the area contains many synagogues and religious schools which are dedicated to the learning of the Torah and its commentaries.

The citizens of Mea She'arim adhere to a strict code of living, the men being distinguished by their long beards and side locks (see Leviticus 19:27), black clothing and round fur-bordered hats. They speak Yiddish as they believe the Hebrew language should only be used when reading the Scriptures and praying.

They demand modesty in dress from all who visit their

Quarter and rigid observance of the Sabbath (*Shabbat*). Should an unwary motorist enter their streets on such a day their disapproval would probably be expressed by stoning the car!

The Great (Jeshurun) Synagogue

Jeshurun means 'the upright one' and is a poetic name for the people of Israel. This synagogue is the largest in Jerusalem and worthy of a visit. During services the men meet in the main auditorium whilst ladies are seated in the gallery.

Ben Yehuda Street

Eliezer Ben Yehuda, a Lithuanian born in 1858 called for a revival of the Hebrew language in 1880 and devoted his life to that purpose. For 2000 years Hebrew had been the language of religion and not of the people and he was determined to rectify that position.

Settling in Israel he taught the language and started compiling a Hebrew dictionary, creating new words whenever necessary. After his death in 1922 this vast undertaking was carried on by his wife and others, being completed 25 years later in 16 volumes.

Jerusalem mourned for three days after his death and is not the only City to honour his memory with a Ben Yehuda street or precinct. With its cafes, restaurants, shops and tradesmen the Street especially comes alive once Shabbat has ended.

Mount Herzl

Theodore Herzl (1860–1904) was an Hungarian Jewish journalist who was dedicated to seeing a legally established homeland for all Jews. His book *The Jewish State* was published in 1896 and the following year he convened the first Zionist Congress in Basle when the Jewish people were declared to be a nation. This declaration became a fact 50 years later! He is buried on Mount Herzl where there is a replica of the study in Vienna where he worked.

Israel Museum – The Shrine of the Book

The Israel Museum is actually a complex of several museums containing a vast wealth of art, sculpture, archaeological and parchment treasures. Many, many hours can be spent drinking in the wonders of this superb collection of precious exhibits.

The Shrine of the Book is unique as it contains the Dead Sea Scrolls discovered at Qumran from 1947. The building is quite distinctive in that it is fashioned after the top of one of the jars that contained many of the scrolls. Perhaps one of the most exciting finds was a complete scroll of the book of Isaiah said to be 1000 years earlier than any other previous copy.

Jerusalem Model

Constructed in the grounds of the Holyland Hotel in West Jerusalem this fascinating (1 in 50) scale-model of Jerusalem at the time of Jesus is extremely helpful and instructive especially in depicting the Temple complex.

The Yad Vashem Holocaust Memorial

The name *Yad Vashem* means 'Monument and Memorial' and is taken from Isaiah 56:5 where the Lord speaks of establishing within His house a monument and everlasting memorial. It commemorates the tragic loss of six million Jews who were slaughtered at the hands of the Nazis in the Second World War.

There is an Exhibition Hall containing written, photographic and filmed records and an extensive collection of books and resource materials; the Hall of Names holds the register of holocaust victims. The central feature is the stark simplicity of the Hall of Remembrance where burns the Eternal Flame. Inscribed on the floor are the names of the twenty-one most prominent death and concentration camps.

Hadassah Medical Centre – Chagall Windows

The Hadassah is the largest hospital in the Middle East.

Included in the complex is a synagogue containing the famous Marc Chagall windows, each one being devoted to one of the twelve tribes of Israel.

Ein Kerem

Although not mentioned by name in the gospel account there are historical records to show that Ein Kerem (Spring of the Vineyards) was the birth-place of John the Baptist and the home of Zechariah and Elizabeth.

This is where Mary came after being visited by the angel Gabriel and told the amazing news that she was to be the mother of the longed-for Messiah, the Son of God. She was also told that her relative Elizabeth was already six months pregnant despite being well-advanced in years! The first chapter of Luke's gospel gives the background story.

The Church of the Visitation commemorates the time Mary and Elizabeth spent together whilst the Church of St. John marks the traditional site of the home where John was born. A seemingly unrelated Scripture is given added force when viewed in the light of the meeting and sharing together of these two women.

Think back a moment to the fifteenth chapter of John's gospel. A few hours before Jesus was arrested in Gethsemane He teaches the disciples the absolute necessity of believers being in a vital, living relationship with Him. Using the illustration of the vine He shows that just as the branches need to remain in it in order to grow and produce fruit so it is imperative for believers (branches) to remain in Him (the Vine) and His words to remain in them.

The word linking this passage to the meeting of the two expectant mothers is 'remain', although the word 'abide' as used in the King James version carries a far richer meaning – *'and Mary abode with her* (Elizabeth) *about three months ...'* (Luke 1:56).

Can you imagine the excitement and endless talk as they discussed their futures and all the implications of mother-hood? The changes, the challenges, the commitments! They must have had a positive involvement with each other and a communion and fellowship at the deepest level. That is the meaning of 'abiding' and that's exactly what Jesus is saying regarding our relationship to Him and His Word. John 15:7 says,

> *If you abide in me and my words abide in you, ask whatever you wish and it will be given you.*

That word 'ask' is written in the imperative tense which really means *'I challenge you ... '*; 'anything' actually indicates 'the merest thought'. So Jesus is virtually saying He challenges believers to ask for even the things in their merest thoughts!

That almost sounds like signing an open cheque – but He knows that when we are really abiding in Him, and His words and teaching are abiding in us we shall only ever want those things that will enable us to glorify Him.

Use your visit to re-appraise your own situation.

Ein Kerem

Let My words live in you, let their roots go deep
    inside,
Let My words grow in you, let their truths in you
    abide,
Then your thoughts will start to change as you open
    up your mind
And your actions and your life will start to be like
    mine.
    Then you'll find you'll want to do
    All the things I've taught you to,
    And your trust in what I've taught
    Will produce the life it ought.

    Here's My promise, here's My Word,
    Whate'er you ask, it will be heard,
    It will be done, the answer's sure,
    Abide in Me and doubt no more.

The Mount of Olives

According to a Jewish tradition the Messiah will come from the east passing the Mount of Olives, cross the Kidron Valley and enter the Temple. Jesus did exactly that 2000 years ago! They believe all the dead will rise at that time, those on the Mount of Olives being the first; this perhaps explains why the western slopes of the Mount appear to be a gigantic cemetery. By contrast the Muslim belief is that those buried nearest to the City wall in the Kidron Valley will be the first to rise.

Bethany

Nestling at the foot of the eastern slopes of the Mount of Olives, Bethany was the home of Martha and Mary and their brother Lazarus. It literally means 'the House of Dates' but the Arabs still call it 'the Home of Lazarus' and there is a well-preserved rock-chamber tomb around which the village has grown. Bethany reminds us of the busyness of Martha (Luke 10:40), the raising of Lazarus from the dead (John 11), and the anointing of Jesus by Mary (John 12).

> Bethany, sweet Bethany,
> A home that was so dear to me,
> A place of comfort, love and peace
> where I could rest, and find release.
>
> Dear Martha, always on the go
> in cooking, serving – all to show
> the greatest hospitality,
> If only...
> If only she'd spent much more time with Me!
>
> Sweet Mary, quiet and thoughtful too,
> Supporting all I sought to do,
> Believing, hoping, keen to learn
> of Father's Kingdom; keen to spurn
> the things that weren't of lasting good –
> She feasted on my heavenly food!

And then dear Lazarus, brother true,
Upholding all his sisters tried to do;
Struck down in death! Dismay, despair,
Dear Martha cries, 'If you'd been there
my brother would be living still!'
Her faith proclaimed her trust was real.

I am the Resurrection, child believe all that I say,
I am Eternal Life, I am the Truth, I am the Way;
My Father will be glorified, His will on earth be done,
His power will be manifest in the Person of His Son.

So Lazarus 'Come forth' – He lives!
Come, let your life declare
the answer that my Father gives
to all believing prayer.

An incident recorded in Mark 14:3–9 reveals something of Mary's heart of love that can be an encouragement to all believers.

She had an alabaster jar containing a very expensive perfume. Alabaster was a costly material (the windows of All Nations Church, Gethsemane are made of alabaster) but the perfume – nard, from India – was far more costly, worth in the region of a labourer's wage for a whole year! She broke the jar and used all the contents to anoint Jesus. He sees her act as symbolic of His approaching death and burial; Judas sees it as an extravagance and misuse of money.

Perhaps we are like Mary's gift. Her container was precious but it needed to be broken before the real value and worth of her gift could be realised. All of us are precious in God's sight but as we allow our wills to be lovingly broken by His will for us – as we pray constantly to be filled by His Spirit, we are told,

God manifests through us the sweet aroma of the knowledge of Jesus in every place. (2 Corinthians 2:14, 15 NASB)

We become a fragrance of Jesus to God both amongst believers and unbelievers. That is precious to Father! And the fragrance (the aroma) becomes more precious as we allow our lives to be moulded by His Word. If we get a grip upon it so that it gets a grip upon our lives, it will ensure our love, our worship, our service is not counterfeit but like Mary's perfume, pure.

Bethphage

Climb the Mount from Bethany to the village of Bethphage (the House of the Unripe, or Juiceless, Fig). Whether or not this was *'the village ahead of you ... '* (Matthew 21:2) this is where the Church commemorates that first Palm Sunday procession.

Every year this exciting event is re-enacted starting from the church and, reaching the summit of the Mount of Olives, descends past the churches of the Pater Noster, Dominus Flevit and All Nations to cross the Kidron Valley, entering the Old city through St. Stephen's Gate. However, pause a while at Bethphage and meditate on the importance and impact of this great event.

Jesus had come to Bethany accompanied by a great crowd of pilgrims who were going up to Jerusalem for the Feast of Passover. After staying with His dear friends at Bethany He is ready to enter the great City and He chooses to do so on a young donkey.

We see this as a dramatic fulfilment of Zechariah 9:9, and it's possible some of the pilgrims feel the same way for they start to get excited and shout *'Hosanna (Save now) Son of David, Blessed is He who comes in the name of the Lord!'*

> *Rejoice greatly, O Daughter of Zion!*
> *Shout, daughter of Jerusalem!*
> *See, your king comes to you,*
> *righteous and having salvation,*
> *gentle and riding on a donkey,*
> *on a colt, the foal of a donkey.*

Can we learn anything from that young donkey so far as serving the Lord is concerned? Certainly it was **available** –

and Jesus knew it! Can the same be said of us? In establishing His great plan of salvation, it was necessary for God to make Jesus available to us in order to become our Sin-bearer; He carried the whole weight and burden of our sin to Calvary.

Once we are prepared to admit our need of salvation God makes His Holy Spirit available to us so that we can receive His gift of eternal life. Having done that we become members of His family and now He wants us to be available to **Him** in all sorts of ways. So here's another thought.

The donkey was **adaptable**. We could assume its young life had been spent in eating, playing and sleeping – it had certainly never been ridden (Mark 11:2), yet in the hands of Jesus it was able to cope with change and adapt to something quite new.

Sometimes we find ourselves facing alternative actions and having to make choices and decisions. When God challenges you to make a change remember that He will always supply the necessary grace and ability, and equip you to work efficiently and easily under His loving hand!

Mosque of the Ascension

Originally a 4th Century church that was reconstructed by the Crusaders, it has remained in Muslim hands since the time of Saladin. It contains 'a footprint of Jesus' which is a reminder of His ascension into heaven (although Luke 24:50 says this occurred in the vicinity of Bethany). It is a reminder too, of His Second Coming recorded in Acts 1:11 and prophesied in Zechariah 14:4:

> *On that day his feet will stand on the Mount of Olives, east of Jerusalem, and the Mount of Olives will be split in two from east to west, forming a great valley, with half of the mountain moving north and half moving south.*

Church of the Pater Noster

As you see the scores of languages depicting the prayer that binds the nations of the world together, remember it is also a lovely pattern on which to base our private prayers. Praying this great prayer publicly is wonderfully edifying when prayed from the heart; but don't be content. Use it as a spring-board into greater mysteries of prayer that will unlock the windows of heaven and shower you with amazing answers.

Church of Dominus Flevit (Jesus Wept)

Commemorating the traditional site where Jesus wept over Jerusalem (Luke 19:41–44 – yet how often He must have done so!) the roof of this lovely little church is in the form of a tear-drop. The front of the altar bears a striking mosaic of a hen with her chicks (Matthew 23:37).

> 'Oh my people, Oh my people
> Won't you listen, watch and see,
> The things I teach are straight from God,
> Let me your Teacher be.
> Yet constantly you turn your back
> Refusing love and grace;
> And yet I came from Father,
> To share His love's embrace.
>
> The days are fast approaching, the enemy's at the
> door,
> Your hearts will break, you'll wait and mourn
> Your City is no more!
>
> Jerusalem, Jerusalem, if you had only known
> That God in me had come to earth to claim His very
> own!'

(Within 40 years the Romans had overrun the City and the Temple was destroyed.)

Gethsemane (Oil Press)

At the foot of the western slopes of the Mount and overlooking the Kidron valley lies Gethsemane with its two churches. The Russian Church of St. Mary Magdalene with its seven golden onion-shaped domes was consecrated in 1888.

The newer Church of the Agony is more popularly known as the Church of All Nations. Consecrated in 1924, many nations contributed to the building of this beautiful church with its twelve cupolas and magnificent pictures in coloured and gilt mosaics. Diffused light enters through windows of alabaster revealing the Rock of Agony which is said to be the place where Jesus overcame every temptation to avoid the way of the Cross.

(Gethsemane is also mentioned in the Section 'The Final Hours'.)

In and Around the Old City

Bethesda

Entering the Old City by the eastern gate (known variously as St. Stephen's, Lion, Sheep, and St. Mary's Gate), a door on the right leads into the grounds of St. Anne's Church. Built on the site of the traditional home of the Virgin Mary's parents, Anna and Joachim, it is charming in its simplicity and is a very fine example of Crusader architecture. The wonderful echo needs testing to be believed!

In the same grounds are the excavations of Bethesda (House of Mercy), the 'pool near the Sheep Gate' recorded in John 5. Here is where the man who had been an invalid for 38 years was healed by Jesus, an act that incurred the wrath of the Jewish leaders because it was performed on the Sabbath!

The road continues into the **Via Dolorosa** which see under the section 'The Final Hours'.

Pool of Siloam

Returning through St. Stephen's Gate and moving down the Kidron Valley another pool is reached that witnessed a healing miracle. John 9 records Jesus anointing a blind man's eyes with mud and telling him to *'Go, wash in the Pool of Siloam.'* Through obeying Jesus his eyesight was restored!

Another reference to this Pool appears under 'Succot' in Part IV.

Hezekiah's Tunnel

The most exciting way to visit the Pool of Siloam is through this ancient tunnel. In Bible times the Gihon Spring was outside the City walls causing the inhabitants to be vulnerable to a besieging army. To rectify this, King Hezekiah (about 700 BC) instructed his engineers to bore a tunnel from the spring to the Pool, an actual distance of about 1100 feet.

In practice, they worked simultaneously from both ends and despite having meandered somewhat met almost exactly in the middle having covered a distance of some 1777 feet! An inscription recording this great engineering feat was discovered near the outlet of the tunnel in 1880 and is now preserved in an Instanbul museum.

Those intending to use the tunnel should take torches and be prepared to wade through water, especially in late Spring and Summer-time.

The Golden Gate

This is the only gate in the eastern wall of the City and it is blocked up! By tradition, it is the gateway used by Jesus on the first Palm Sunday.

In Crusader times it was only opened twice a year and one of these was when the Palm Sunday procession (complete with palm branches) descended from the Mount of Olives and entered the City. The northern arch is called the Gate of Repentance and the southern one the Gate of Mercy.

In 1530 it was completely blocked up by the Turks; some believe it will only be opened again when Jesus returns.

Montefiore Windmill – Yemin Moshe

Sir Moses Montefiore, the British philanthropist visited Israel a number of times between 1827 and 1875, founding the first housing development outside the City walls in 1860. His aim was to ease the congestion and poor living conditions in the Old City.

 He built a windmill to serve the needs of new settlements but the lack of wind meant it became more of a landmark and is today a museum beside the house where he lived. An inscription proclaims him as Founder of New Jerusalem.

Mount Zion

Looking eastwards from the Montefiore Windmill, the **Dormition** ('Sleep of St. Mary') **Abbey** dominates the skyline of Mount Zion. Consecrated in 1906, the Abbey marks the traditional site where the mother of Jesus died.

Nearby is **King David's Tomb**, said to be the sepulchre of the greatest of all the Jewish kings. Revered by the Jews as second in importance only to the Western Wall there is considerable doubt that this is no more than an imposing memorial.

The Old Testament records in 1 Kings 2:10 that David was buried in the City of David and this was located south of the Temple area on Mount Ophel.

The upper storey is the **Cenacle** ('Upper Chamber') believed by some to be the Upper Room where Jesus held His last Passover, instituting the Last Supper and where subsequently the miracle of Pentecost occurred. Whilst there is doubt concerning its authenticity (and as a site perhaps quite disappointing) it is an opportunity to be reminded of the important events it commemorates.

Jaffa Gate

This gate was opened to its present size in 1898 to allow the German Kaiser Wilhelm 11 to pass through in his carriage. By contrast, when General Allenby captured Jerusalem in

1917 he insisted on dismounting from his horse saying he would not ride into the City of his Saviour.

The Citadel

To the right of the Jaffa Gate is the Citadel, the Tower of David, built on the remains of Herod's Palace. It houses an extremely fine and ambitious museum that should be visited.

Christ Church

Inside Jaffa Gate is Christ Church, the first Protestant church in Jerusalem. Founded by the Christian Mission to the Jews in 1849 it incorporates some of the features of a synagogue which has caused it to be known as the Jewish church. The complex includes a guest house, coffee shop and book shop.

Damascus Gate

In the centre of the northern wall of the Old City this is the busiest of all the gates and provides easy access to the Moslem and Christian Quarters.

Solomon's Quarry

Just to the east of Damascus Gate is the entrance to an immense quarry that extends about 700 feet under the Old City. It is likely this area yielded some of the vast quantity of stone used in the building of Solomon's Temple.

It is also known as Zedekiah's Cave as legend maintains this last King of Judah used the cave to escape from the Babylonians only to be captured in the plains of Jericho.

St. George's Cathedral

From Damascus Gate the Nablus Road stretches north and no traveller can fail to see the very English Cathedral which is the seat of the Anglican Archbishop. Built in 1898 it is interesting that it contains both a font and an open baptistery.

Tombs of the Kings

Despite its name this has nothing to do with any king! It belonged to Queen Helen of Adiabene in Mesopotamia who, coming to Jerusalem in AD 45 with her family, converted to Judaism. They were all buried here and the sarcophagus of the Queen was discovered in 1863. At the entrance to the tombs is a fine example of a rolling stone.

Bethlehem and the Judean Wilderness

Rachel's Tomb

Rachel, the wife of Jacob and mother of Joseph died giving birth to Benjamin. Her tomb has become a most holy site for both Muslim and Jews. Housed in a building enlarged by Sir Moses Montefiore many women will pray here to be blessed in child-birth.

Bethlehem

In Hebrew, the name '*Beit Lechem*' means 'House of Bread' and it was here that Jesus, who claimed to be the 'Bread of Life' was born!

Jesus is God's Gift of love
Sent to earth from heaven above;
He came down to die for sin,
To touch our hearts and enter in.
He offers cleansing, joy and peace,
And from all worry brings release,
Yet, most of all its **life** He brings
To all who own Him King of kings.
Life Eternal! Here and now!
And hereafter – let us bow
low before Him, and adore
God's own Gift, for evermore!

Although quite an insignificant village the prophet Micah declares,

> *But you, Bethlehem Ephrathah* (fruitfulness) *though you are small among the clans of Judah, out of you will come for me one who will be ruler over Israel, whose origins are from old, from ancient times.*   (Micah 5:2)

Shepherds' Fields

These are perhaps the very fields that once belonged to Boaz, the man who married Ruth the Moabitess. The Old Testament book of her name carries the account of her love and devotion for her mother-in-law Naomi and preserves her time-honoured saying,

> *Don't urge me to leave you or to turn back from you. Where you go I will go, and where you stay I will stay. Your people will be my people and your God my God. Where you die I will die, and there I will be buried. May the Lord deal with me, be it ever so severely, if anything but death separates you and me.*   (Ruth 1:16–17)

How encouraging it is to recall that Ruth, a member of a race who were former enemies of the Israelites became the great-grandmother of David, Israel's greatest king and therefore in direct descent to Jesus Himself, the Saviour of the world and the King of all kings! None are outside the reach of God's love; receiving it is just a matter of faith. (See also **Shavuot** in Part IV.)

More than one site commemorates the Christmas miracle so far as the shepherds are concerned. Caves and chapels embody their story and it is time well spent to meditate upon the wonder of God's love.

What depth of love! Such mystery
That God took on frail flesh for me!

That I, and all who dare believe
in Christ, as Saviour, would receive
Forgiveness! Love! Eternal Life!
Real joy! – and strength to meet all strife,
Let us through all our earthly days
Live lives of heartfelt thanks and praise
to Him who lives for evermore –
    Our **Jesus**!
    Come! Let us adore!

✤ ✤ ✤

Church of the Nativity

Built in the 4th Century on the orders of the Emperor
Constantine this is the oldest church in the world although
it has suffered devastation and consequent restoration over
the many centuries since.

Served by the Greek Orthodox, Latin and Armenian
faiths, it is unlike a church in appearance with entrance
through a low doorway known as the Door of Humility.
Bending to enter is so appropriate for such a significant
place although history tells us that the door's height was
restricted to four feet to prevent invading forces riding into
the church on horseback.

Records dating back to the 2nd Century refer to the cave
where Jesus was born; descending into the Grotto it is
possible to visualise the scene.

It was quite usual in those days for dwellings to be built
as extensions to caves, the latter being warmer in the
winter and cooler in the summer; where the cave was large
it might also have housed animals at night. Perhaps it was
such a cave that accommodated Joseph and Mary on that
crowded, eventful night so long ago?

The silver star beneath the Altar of the Nativity marks
the place where Jesus is said to have been born, and a few
steps away at a lower level the Altar of the Manger where
Jesus was laid – perhaps that part of the cave was shared
with the animals?

The greatest miracle occurred
So many years ago,
The great, eternal loving God
Stepped into history and trod
Our world below.

He came to show us how to live
As on the earth He trod,
He came to give abundant life
And do away with sin and strife
And bring us back to God.

The only way God's plan could work
Was letting His dear Son
Take on Himself our guilt and sin –
Our punishment was laid on Him!
The great and Holy One!

So with the eye of faith believe
That Christmas is the key
to heaven's great salvation plan
to bring together God and man
To share Eternity!

The adjoining church, built in 1882 is the Parish Church of St. Catherine which has often been featured in the televised Christmas Midnight Mass. Stairs from this church lead down to various grottoes and chapels including that of St. Jerome where he lived and studied; perhaps his greatest work was the Vulgate, the Latin translation of the Bible.

On 21st December 1995 the control of Bethlehem was handed over to the Palestinian Authority.

Herodion

This is the volcano-like fortress to the east of Bethlehem. Built by Herod the Great it is 2500 feet above sea level and commands a magnificent view of the Judean Wilderness and down to the Dead Sea. It was one of the last fortresses to fall to the Romans in AD 70 and Herod left orders he should be buried here although his last resting place has never been discovered.

Inn of the Good Samaritan

Although the account of the Good Samaritan is a story illustrating a truth rather than an actual event in history Jesus would have known of inns on the road from Jerusalem to Jericho (Luke 10:30) and this spot had been a stopping place for caravans for many centuries. Certainly the area was a haven for robbers of all descriptions, and travelling the road today still shows how easily they could have surprised the unwary traveller.

The 'inn' was rebuilt as a Turkish Police Post prior to the first World War and used as such by the British during the time of the Mandate. Today it has become a wayside post for souvenir hunters.

Jericho

Said to be the oldest city in the world there were ruins of previous Jerichos here when Joshua came to take this first stronghold in the Promised Land; chapters 1 to 6 of the book of Joshua tell the exciting story.

Built like a vast oasis fed by a life-giving spring, the Old Testament calls this lush, green place the City of Palms, and they abound together with oranges, lemons and bananas. At 800 feet below sea level it enjoys a mild, warm climate.

In the western part of the city across the road from Elisha's Spring (2 Kings 2:19–22) is Tel es-Sultan which covers Joshua's Jericho and westwards from here is the Mount of Temptation traditionally identified with the wilderness temptations of Jesus.

Most of Jericho is now controlled by the Palestinian Authority.

✣ ✣ ✣

The Power of God's Word

The weeks spent in the wilderness
   preparing for your mission,
The hunger, thirst and loneliness,
   fulfilling God's commission,
The time spent in communion,
   absorbing Father's Will,
Fulfilling all of love's command,
   preparing you to heal
the world's dread plight of being lost
   without hope of salvation,
Cut off by sin, oppressed and ruled
   by Satan's domination.
You knew the great extent to which
   redemption's plan would lead,
You saw through Satan's subtlety,
   and so you didn't heed
his call to turn the stones to bread,
   to tempt the Lord your God,
Nor offer worship to this one
   who held man 'neath his rod,
You challenged him with Scripture,
   you met his every blow,
You proved God's Word is powerful,
   that it can overthrow
whatever Satan tries to do
   to bring God's people down –
**We'll strive to stand in victory on Scripture's solid
   ground!**

✛ ✛ ✛

Qumran

The name indicates this is the 'Land of the two Moons' due
to the reflection in the Dead Sea when the moon is
shining. A certain air of mysticism pervades the site that
many believe was inhabited by the Essenes, a group of

Jewish priests who broke away from the control of the high priesthood and Temple ritual around 150 BC.

Leading a monastic life-style they spent much time studying and copying the Scriptures. When they realised they would be overrun by the advancing Roman army in 63 BC they hid all their library of scrolls in nearby caves where a vast hoard was discovered in 1947 with further finds in 1956.

Ein Gedi

> *He turned the desert into pools of water*
> *and the parched ground into flowing springs.*
>
> (Psalm 107:35)

Lying on the western coast of the Dead Sea amongst miles of barren cliff and undulating wilderness is Ein Gedi – 'the Fountain of the Kid'. First mentioned in the Bible as part of Judah's inheritance it became better known as the stronghold used by David when hiding from King Saul and where on one occasion he spared Saul's life (1 Samuel 24).

This oasis in the desert, complete with waterfall has become a magnificent Nature Reserve with scores of plants and animals, the most prominent of the latter being the ibex which has been adopted as the symbol of the Israel Nature Reserves Authority.

God is in the Wilderness

In the emptiness of desert, in the arid waste of sand,
In the stretches of dry barrenness we see God's
   mighty hand;
   For He makes the desert bloom and live,
   His hand controls each grain;
   Each particle of earth and grit
   Is part of His domain.

Are you finding life a wilderness,
   does nothing seem worthwhile,

Is each day pointless – empty,
  is each step you take, a trial?
Be honest with your feelings and be honest with the
    Lord,
Cry out to Him for rescue, look to Him to bring
    reward;
For in loneliness He comforts and His Presence brings
    a glow;
In hopelessness He gives new hope, He causes springs
    to flow
producing life and colour; vitality and health;
transforming gloom and poverty into lives of untold
    wealth.

Don't let your life be barren
Nor resist God's holy Will,
Let His healing streams of water
Deal with all that makes you ill.

✢ ✢ ✢

Masada

Eleven miles beyond Ein Gedi and rising like a proud ship
some 1400 feet above the south-west coast of the Dead Sea
is Masada. Once a winter palace cum fortress for Herod the
Great it was captured by Jewish Zealots around AD 66.

When Jerusalem fell to the Romans four years later,
many thousands of the inhabitants were massacred and
many more taken captive. A few hundred escaped and
joined the Zealots on Masada, a total of about 1000 souls;
they managed to hold out against 10,000 Roman soldiers
for three years!

Masada can be climbed by the Snake Path or the easier
ramp on the western side; however, the majority prefer the
cable car! Buy the booklet at the site and read the amazing
story that inspires modern-day Israelis to survive at all
costs.

Hebron

One of the oldest cities in the world, it has a long and rich Jewish history which sadly has been marred by claims and counter-claims concerning ownership causing untold heartache and bloodshed. Ironically, its name comes from the Hebrew *'haver'* meaning 'friend'.

Biblical interest centres around the Cave of Machpela which Genesis 23 tells us was bought by Abraham from Ephron the Hittite for 400 shekels of silver, a fact brought to the attention of the United Nations in 1971 by Chaim Herzog, the Israeli UN Ambassador. He asked for the relevant verses to be circulated to the Council to support the claim that the City was Jewish despite its large Arab majority.

It had been given to Caleb (Joshua 14:13) and became one of the Cities of Refuge. It was here David was anointed king and resided for the first seven years of his long reign.

King Herod built the stone structure over the Cave and the Byzantines and Crusaders transformed it into a church. After the Crusaders were evicted the Moslem Mameluke Sultan Beibars transformed it into a mosque and Jews were forbidden to approach nearer than the seventh step leading to the main entrance.

Jews lived in the City almost continuously throughout the Byzantine, Arab, Mameluke and Ottoman periods but in 1929 sixty-seven of their number were murdered by Arabs and the rest were forced to leave. Synagogues were desecrated and Torah scrolls burned; there was no Jewish population until after the Six Day War in 1967 when the first Jew to enter the Cave was Rabbi Shlomo Goren, the Chief Chaplain of the Israel Defence Forces.

Since 1970 there has been a Jewish settlement built on the ridge above the Cave overlooking the City, called by the biblical name Kiryat Arba meaning the Town of the Four, a reference to the four Patriarchs buried in the Cave; Abraham (and Sarah), Isaac (and Rebecca), Jacob (and Leah) and (by tradition) Adam (and Eve). Jewish belief is that when Joseph's bones were brought back from Egypt they were also buried here.

For years Hebron has been the centre of riots and unmasked hatred between both contenders for ownership and for this reason most tourist groups no longer visit the City which apart from its biblical significance is well-known for its glass-blowing and the manufacture of leather (goatskin) goods.

On 25th February 1994 a Jewish doctor, Baruch Gold-stein went berserk in the Cave opening fire on Muslim worshippers, killing 29 and wounding a further 125.

Discussion, argument and debate marked with outbreaks of hatred and violence continues. On 17th January 1997 the Palestinian Authority was given control of 80% of Hebron; many of their number demand that the remaining Jewish families leave – the latter are equally adamant living in what they maintain is rightfully theirs.

Beersheva

The biblical Beersheva was the place where Abraham made a Covenant of Peace with Abimelech, the Philistine king of Gerar. As proof of having dug a well there, the Patriarch gave the king seven ewe lambs (Genesis 21:22–32). The name means 'Well of the Oath' although it can also mean the 'Well of Seven'. It was once Israel's most southerly town, hence the expression 'from Dan to Beersheva' denoting the north-south boundaries of the Land.

Known today as the Capital of the Negev with a great emphasis on educational facilities and thriving industrial businesses, it has become the trading centre for thousands of Bedouins many of whom have settled there permanently.

Travelling North to Galilee

The quickest route is via Jericho along the Jordan Valley to Beit She'an. The central route through Judea and Samaria (now West Bank) is jointly under Israeli/Palestinian control and at present many groups do not use this way. However those who do have the opportunity of travelling via the valley of Lebonah to Jacob's Well (Nablus – Old Testament Shechem) and Samaria.

Lebonah

The valley of Luban (the biblical Lebonah) contains a broad and fruitful area known as the 'Plain of the Maidens' or the 'Valley of the Dancers'. To the north-east is Seilun which identifies the ancient, but important town of Shiloah. It was here the Ark of the Covenant remained until captured by the Philistines (Joshua 18:1 & 1 Samuel 4).

Once a year the daughters of Shiloah would dance in the valley in honour of the Lord and it was on one such occasion that some of the tribe of Benjamin took the opportunity of claiming wives for themselves (see Judges 19–21 for the terrible story that results in this happier ending).

Nablus

An important West Bank town that includes about 500 Samaritans; they believe they are the descendants of the tribes of Ephraim, Manasseh and some of the Levites. They have a copy of the Torah which is said to date from the time of Joshua commanding the children of Israel to build their Temple on Mount Gerizim. The traditional Passover sacrifice is still observed there each year.

Mount Gerizim lies to the south-west of Nablus while Mount Ebal is to the north. These two places were featured in God's command to Moses concerning the reciting of the blessings on Gerizim and the cursings on Ebal when they had come into the Promised Land. Under Joshua's leadership they carried out this command, marching nearly 40 miles in order to do so! (See Deuteronomy 11:26–32; also Chronicles 27 & 28 and Joshua 8:33–34.)

Jacob's Well

There is mention of a church on this site in the time of St. Jerome and several have been erected and destroyed since then. The Well which is about 120 feet deep has outlasted them all and still provides refreshing water. John chapter 4 shows how skilfully Jesus used it to speak to the Samaritan woman about Eternal Life.

Samaria

Omri the sixth king of Israel built Samaria which became the capital of the Northern Kingdom of Israel. Later, his son Ahab built a temple to the heathen god Baal.

Prophets foretold the city's destruction which was brought about by the Assyrians in 721 BC after a three years siege.

The Romans rebuilt it in 27 BC and Caesar Augustus gave it to Herod who enlarged and embellished it, naming it Sebaste (Greek for Augustus). Is this the city where crowds witnessed the Spirit of God at work under Philip's preaching (Acts 8)?

Using the alternative coastal route means travelling westwards from Jerusalem making possible visits to, for example:

The Cave of Sorek

This is Samson and Delilah country. The cave was discovered by accident during quarry blasting in the area and contains the most breath-taking stalactites and stalagmites of anywhere in Israel.

Abu Ghosh

This is the biblical Kiryat Jearim where the Ark of the Covenant, having been returned by the Philistines, was stranded for 20 years until David took it to Jerusalem, his new capital (1 Samuel 6 & 2 Samuel 6). It was kept in Abinadab's house, and a modern church built on the hill is claimed to be erected over that site; it guards a giant statue of the Madonna and Child and is known as the Church of our Lady of the Ark of the Covenant.

Some maintain a finer church is the Crusader one erected over the spring (where the Romans before them had built a reservoir) believing the village to be the gospel Emmaus.

El Qubeiba

An alternative site for Emmaus, one which has held favour for over 400 years. The Franciscan church is nearly 100 years old but built on Crusader foundations; the left-hand nave is thought to incorporate the remains of a wall of the house of Cleopas (Luke 24:13–35). An 'orientation graph' on a platform to the side of the church will help you check your bearings!

Latrun

Lying in the Ayalon valley this is where some of the fiercest battles were fought in Israel's War of Independence in 1948. It was under Jordanian rule from 1948–67.

Situated on the main highway is the Trappist monastery of Latrun. Its origins go back to 1890 although work on the monastery didn't commence until 1927. Renowned for its wine-making the Order is one that observes long fasts and poverty. No talking is permitted in the church, library or dining-room except by the Abbot.

Caesarea

Founded about 600 BC Herod the Great transformed it into a magnificent city around 22 BC and 12 years later named it Caesarea after Caesar Augustus. It became the official residence of the Roman procurators of Judea who went up to Jerusalem with their troops at Festival times or in an emergency.

This is the city where the Roman centurion received a visit from Peter (Acts 10). Philip the Evangelist lived here with his four daughters and it is where Paul was imprisoned for two years.

Prior to 1961 the only factual evidence of the existence of Pontius Pilate was the Gospel account and that of Josephus. However, whist excavating the site of the Roman theatre a stone was unearthed bearing the names Pilatus and Augustus (Caesar) which effectively silenced the voices of the critics! A copy of the stone can be seen in the theatre grounds.

Megiddo

Standing at the head of a mountain pass Megiddo guards access to the north from the coastal plains as well as the east/west road across the valley. Its strategic position means it featured frequently in battles over the centuries.

Excavations have revealed evidence of some 20 different civilisations from around 4000 to 400 BC. Of especial interest is the huge grain silo and the great tunnel bored through the rock that brought water into the fortress from a spring in the plain.

In 1917 the Allied armies under General Allenby entered northern Palestine through the Megiddo Pass driving out the Turks. When created a peer, the General assumed the title of Viscount Allenby of Megiddo.

Mentioned in Revelation 16, Har Megiddo (the Hill of Megiddo) becomes Armageddon, the site of the last great battle.

Ein Harod

The story of Gideon and the reduction of his army from 32,000 to 300 and God's subsequent victory is contained in Judges 7. Ein Harod (the Spring of Harod) is where they camped; today it feeds into a very attractive open-air swimming pool.

Beit Alpha

It was here in 1928 that a beautiful mosaic floor was discovered belonging to a 6th century AD synagogue. It has been carefully restored and is well worth a visit.

Gan Hashlosha (the Garden of the Three)

A very attractive and ideal place for a picnic and swimming with three connected fresh-water pools and waterfalls.

Beit She'an (House of Rest)

A third-century Rabbi is recorded as saying, 'If paradise is situated in the Land of Israel, its entrance is in Beit Shean', words prompted no doubt by the then abundance of water nourishing a fertile soil. It is the town where the decapitated bodies of King Saul and his sons were displayed (1 Samuel 31).

In more recent times it was deserted by the Arabs in 1948 and is now the principal Jewish centre in the Jordan Valley. It boasts a second-century Roman theatre seating 5000 and as a result of excavations in recent years there is emerging what is said to be the best preserved – and largest – Roman city in the country.

El-Muhraka (Sacrifice)

At a height of around 2000 feet on the southernmost point of the Carmel ridge is Muhraka, the traditional spot where God through His servant Elijah confounded the prophets of Baal (1 Kings 18). Their subsequent execution is said to have been carried out in the Kishon Valley.

Haifa

Sometimes known as the capital of the north it is the country's chief port. Days can be spent exploring here but if you are passing through, a stop on Panorama Road is essential; the view is truly breath-taking.

Halfway down the Carmel slope is the big golden dome of the Bahai Temple. Thousands of centres in different countries cater for about 4.5 million Bahais; there is only a small community in Israel despite Haifa being its World Centre.

Bahai means 'glory' and the faith developed out of a Muslim mystical movement founded in Persia (1844) where it was prohibited. Bahais welcome the wisdom of all great religious leaders but are regarded by most Muslims as heretics. Named after its prophet Baha-Ulla he was exiled to Acre in 1868 by the Turks who kept him prisoner for 24 years.

Acre

Originally called Akko, it was renamed Ptolemais when captured by the Ptolemies of Egypt. Its main history began with the Crusades in 1104; it became the main seaport of the Christian Kingdom and an important trade and commercial centre.

When the Knights Hospitallers of St. John became established in the city the name was changed to St. John of Acre; a visit to the underground city is a must.

The Moslem leader El Jazzar (the butcher) defended the town against Napoleon in 1799 with the help of the British fleet. Napoleon retreated to Egypt and El Jazzar murdered all the wounded. The mosque was built in 1781/2.

Central Galilee

Tiberias

Tiberias, the Capital of Galilee, was built in AD 17 by one of Herod the Great's sons, Herod Antipas. He was the man who had John the Baptist beheaded to satisfy a foolhardy oath he had made to the daughter of his unlawful wife Herodias (Mark 6:14:29).

Built during the lifetime of Jesus to honour the Roman emperor Tiberias, the area was already famous throughout the Roman world for the health-giving properties of its hot springs.

After Jerusalem was destroyed by the Romans in AD 70, Tiberias became a religious centre of learning for the Jews, and around AD 200 it became the seat of the Sanhedrin Council. The Jewish Talmud was produced here which consists of the Mishna (the Jewish Oral Law) and the Gemara, a commentary on and complementary to the Mishna.

Just to the south of the town is the excavation of the ancient town of Hammat (from the Hebrew *'cham'* – 'hot') and famous for its hot springs. Here the beautiful mosaics of a 1st century synagogue were restored in 1965; they are the same images and signs as those at Beit Alpha.

Nearby is the tomb of the wise Rabbi Meir Ba'al Haness whilst in Tiberias itself the tomb of the great 12th Century Jewish physician and philosopher Maimonides (Moses ben Maimon) deserves a visit. He was affectionately known as the Rambam.

Cana

About 16 miles west of Tiberias and some four miles before reaching Nazareth is the present village of Kfar Kana – said to produce the best pomegranates in Israel! It is occupied by Arabs, both Christian and Moslem. The Greek Orthodox church bears a white dome whilst the red-domed Franciscan parish church is believed to be built on the remains of the house where the 'water into wine' miracle occurred.

The second chapter of John's gospel will remind you of the event and some couples take the opportunity of renewing their marriage vows here. In this connection it may be helpful to look at three words that appear in the fifth chapter of Ephesians; they are 'be united', 'love' and 'submit'.

'Be united' (v. 31) is part of a quotation from Genesis 2:24 and comes from the Old English word 'cleave'. Its root meaning is 'to be securely glued together' or in today's language 'superglued'. It is certain that when God initiated marriage He intended it should be a permanent relationship!

'Love' (v. 25) which speaks of the love a husband should have for his wife, likens it to that of Jesus for His Church. The Scriptural word used is *'agape'* love, a love that is bestowed upon people because they are precious, a love that will sacrifice everything – including life itself! – for the sake of those who are loved **even when love is not shown in return**! It is in the light of such a self-giving love that God says to wives 'submit'.

'Submit' (v. 22) is not the hard word it's made out to be. It is rooted in a military term meaning 'having a defined freedom under authority'. In other words a wife has many opportunities to use her gifts, talents and abilities within the marriage union – but God holds the man responsible for the marriage and welfare of the family.

If he constantly bestows upon his wife a love that is so expressive, tender and consuming that he would sacrifice anything for her happiness, wellbeing and security – how special she would feel! How exciting and satisfying to be in such a union! For her, submission would mean loving security!

However, we mustn't overlook the miracle that took place at Cana's wedding feast and all of us can benefit from dwelling on the great truths it illustrates. For just as the water was turned into wine so the touch of Jesus will transform the tasteless into the extraordinary; it will bring colour into the drab and dull, and a warmth and richness into a life that is cold and offering little. Jesus transforms everything by the touch of His love and power.

To what extent have we allowed Him to transform our lives?

> Jesus, by the touch of your loving Presence you can
> completely change the listless life into one that is
> vibrant and active; you can bring colour and
> excitement into that which is unattractive and dull;
> you can inject warmth and richness into a cold and
> lifeless existence. Place within us by your Holy Spirit
> a desire to be touched by your hand of power every
> day.

Nazareth

This town had a negative reputation in the time of Jesus giving rise to the saying *'Can any good thing come out of Nazareth?'* (John 1:46). Today it is occupied by Moslem and Christian Arabs whilst to the north-east is the much newer Jewish town known as Nazareth Heights.

With much to see the central place of interest must be the new (Franciscan) Church of the Annunciation

completed in 1965 and built upon the traditional home of
Mary and the place where the angel gave her the staggering
news she was to be the mother of the promised Messiah –
God's own Son!

Mary

Dear Mary, sweet and innocent, an unsuspecting
    child,
Shielded through those early years, kept pure and
    undefiled,
Gentle, honest, open; and fit for God's own use,
For an unimagined purpose, for an act none could
    deduce;
To be God's special vehicle! To bring about His plan,
She would become a mother – but not through
    earthly man.
Her Child would be conceived by God, **His** Infant
    without sin,
Pure, righteous, having all the attributes of God –
    within
a human frame! What wonder, that such a thing
    could be,
A holy God, for love of man, stepped into history,
To be the means of buying back from Satan's deathly
    power,
Those whom He had created, on whom He'd planned
    to shower
a sacrificial, vibrant love that would not let them go,
Whoever in their rightful mind could ever say Him
    'no'?

Beit She'arim (House of Gates)

This lies at the western edge of the Jezreel valley and by the
3rd Century had become a prominent Jewish city and
the seat of the Sanhedrin Council before its removal to

Tiberias. The scholarly and much revered Rabbi Yehuda
Hanassi who compiled the Mishna lived here.

Following the destruction of Jerusalem the Jews were no
longer able to bury their dead on the Mount of Olives and
because of Rabbi Hanassi's association with the city it
became their central burial place. Some of the catacombs
can be visited as well as other archaeological finds (a
synagogue, olive press, church). The town was destroyed
in the 4th Century AD and virtually forgotten until
excavations commenced in 1936.

Mount Tabor

At 300 feet above sea-level Tabor rises 1500 feet like a giant
hedgehog in an otherwise flat field. Resting on the south-
west plain of Jezreel (Esdraelon) the area became famous in
Old Testament times for the crushing defeat of the armies of
Sisera by Deborah and Barak. The Lord caused the Kishon
river to flood its banks and Sisera's 900 chariots of iron
became bogged down in the ensuing mud (Judges 4–5).

Nestling at the foot of Tabor is Daburiyah; is this the
village where the disciples were unable to cure the deaf and
dumb boy (Mark 9:14–29)? The ascent starts here via a
number of hairpin bends, the seeming delight of the daring
taxi drivers!

The chapel on its summit was completed in 1924 and is
cared for by the Franciscans. It commemorates the Transfiguration of Jesus in the presence of Peter, James and John.
On this dramatic occasion, the full majesty and splendour
of God's Deity shone out from Jesus causing utter amazement to these, His three closest friends. Moses and Elijah
appeared with Him, too. Read the account in Matthew
17:1–20 and consider this devastating sequel!

In Romans 12:2 we are instructed,

> *Do not conform any longer to the pattern of this world, but
> be transformed by the renewing of your mind.*

This directive becomes breath-taking in its implication in

the light of the transfiguration account. The word Paul uses for 'transformed' is the same word Matthew uses (17:2) for 'transfigured'! God is saying we must not be controlled by the world around us but that we should be transfigured, allowing the love of God to flow out from us! But how? 'By the renewing of your minds...'

We are largely controlled by our thoughts which lead to actions and habits, so we must constantly be renewing our minds – and the best food is God's Word. Read it regularly, meditate upon it, soak it up and allow the Holy Spirit to water it into the depths of your innermost beings. This will enable you to become channels through whom God can manifest the wonder of His love to those around you.

The Jordan River and the Two Seas

The River has three main tributaries – the largest being the Dan – supplemented by the melting snows of Mt Hermon which rises some 8500 feet on Israel's northern border. The River's story is one of continual descent as it flows along this part of the Great Rift Valley dropping around 2500 feet in its first seven miles and a further 920 feet in the next eleven.

Its fresh waters enter the northern shores of the Sea of Galilee which nestles around 600 feet below sea level. Also known as the Sea (Lake) of Tiberias, Gennesaret, Ginnosar and Chinnereth (Hebrew for 'harp-shaped') it measures about 13 miles in length, eight miles at its widest point with just over 32 miles of shore-line. It is 160 feet at its deepest point.

Until the winter of 1991/2 it suffered deprivation through several years of water shortage plus a continual need for irrigating the land and directing water via the National Water Carrier to the arid wastes in the south of the country. Almost a quarter of the nation's water demands are supplied by the Lake which abounds in many types of fish and marine life.

Emergency measures have to be taken when the level of the Lake drops to 212.5 metres below sea level, known as the 'red line' which is an arbitrary figure originally set by the British Mandatory authorities. One reason for establishing this minimum seems to be the presence under the Lake of hot, salt springs which are kept from erupting by the pressure of the water above. If the pressure reduces too much the springs could erupt contaminating this essential fresh-water supply and killing the majority of the fish.

This minimum had practically been reached by the end of 1991 with the Lake having dropped about 13 feet below its optimum level. However, due to torrential rain in December followed by the heaviest snowfalls in living memory plus almost continuous rain for the next two months, the danger was averted.

Experts had predicted that the Sea's normal level could not be regained for some seven to ten years – the Lord decided to do it in as many weeks and the sluice gates in the south of the Lake had to be opened to avoid it overflowing its banks!

It is a beautiful Sea with changing moods and colours, often calm and peaceful but sometimes whipped into violent action by sudden squalls, only to subside once more into quiet inactivity.

Leaving the Sea's southern shore the River meanders down the valley bed towards the Dead Sea but with seeming reluctance as the actual journey of 65 miles covers almost twice that distance. Does it sense its impending doom? Is it aware that its destination spells death as it is received by the Dead Sea lying languidly 1300 feet below sea level, the lowest point on earth?

Apart from some algae no marine life can survive its acrid waters for this Sea gives nothing away willingly. Trapped in a vast depression nearly 50 miles long and 11 miles wide there is no river outlet – but millions of gallons are lost by evaporation every day! The result is that in any given volume of its water, about one third is mineral salt. This produces buoyancy qualities that make floating, or bobbing about like a cork the easiest thing in the world although the heavy mineral content can cause some discomfort and irritation to tender parts of the body.

Yet in the midst of death and pungent odours and a certain morbidity there is untold wealth in the form of calcium, potassium, magnesium and bromide.

The Sea of Galilee

O Sea of moods! Tranquillity,
Of restful blue – and sudden storm
With raging fury, lashing waves
To be replaced by peaceful swells.
The Sea that heard the Master's voice
Addressing crowds across the bay;
That carried to 'the other side'
Disciples, who were following One
Who spoke of love and sacrifice,
Who ruled the storm, commanding winds
To be at rest, be still, be calm!
Who told His men, be full of faith,
Just trust, believe, be unafraid.
The Sea that was the source of life
To thousands living on its shores,
Providing income, food, support,
Security – despite its moods.
The Sea that, leaving by the south
Meanders down the many miles,
Till finally it sheds its life
And, sucked into the Sea of Death
It disappears – it is no more!
Sad Sea, sad River, what an end
To such a fruitful, vital life!
God grant that we might better end
Our days in blessing, still alive
To all that God would have us be,
Deep in His love – tranquillity!

✤ ✤ ✤

Some Memories of Ministry

North from Tiberias, along the western coast of the Sea of Galilee is **Nof Ginossar**, a lakeside kibbutz. It was between here and Migdal that an ancient first-century boat (which some reports chose to call 'the Jesus boat') was discovered in January 1986. It became exposed in the Lake due to a prolonged drought and the Israel Department of Antiquities and Museums, with the help of volunteers mounted a rescue excavation. The Nof Ginossar shows a telling video how the boat was enclosed in polyurethane foam and brought to a conservation pool where it was treated with hot synthetic wax so that it could eventually be exhibited under dry conditions.

Horns of Hittim

A characteristic of the Lake is the occasional, but often quite sudden emergence of storms as evidenced both in Scripture and present day experience. A reason for this could be the combination of two geographical features.

The Lake lies in a deep depression 600 feet below sea level whilst 1200 feet above on its western coast are the Horns of Hittim made famous by Saladin's defeat of the Crusaders in 1187. The area is shaped like an Arabian saddle with its two horns; a wind coming in from the Mediterranean would tend to be compressed between the twin peaks causing it to be speeded up, and then accelerated still further as the hotter air over the low-lying Lake sucks it down causing havoc and chaos to all in its path.

Mount of Beatitudes

About 330 feet above the Lake, the Lord's teaching of the Beatitudes (Matthew 5:1–16) is commemorated in an octagonal church. The eight Beatitudes are inscribed on separate windows and the seven Virtues are inlaid on the floor. The church is cared for by Franciscan sisters who live in the nearby hospice.

How happy are the people who see themselves as spiritually poor – for in Jesus their spiritual wealth knows no bounds! Those that mourn their spiritual poverty will be comforted as they commit their lives to Jesus and revel in His love. Their gentleness will bring them much blessing and as they hunger and thirst after a life that honours God, they will find real satisfaction.

The merciful will receive mercy and those who progressively shun the ways of the world and aim for purity of life will rejoice in increasing revelations of God Himself. The sons of God will promote peace even in the face of the persecution they receive for daring to live a life pleasing to the Lord!

Despite the insults, lies and varied forms of opposition and attack, rejoice and be glad, because your heavenly reward vastly outweighs anything you have lost on earth!

You are the salt of the earth; let your presence in the world bring cleansing and healing. Let it proclaim the flavour of God's love and preserve all that is worthy of His Name. As lights, determine not to be hid; rather let your lives be lived in such a way that all your good works and words will show forth the love of Jesus, so that God will receive all the glory.

Looking out from this vantage point across the loveliness of the countryside and down to the Lake itself, it is easy to visualise the way Jesus took hold of everyday situations and turned them into meaningful teaching aids.

The wheat and weeds growing together (Matthew 13:24–30), the farmer sowing his seed (Mark 4:3–20) and the flocks of sheep following the shepherd as he calls them by name (John 10:27–30) all bring freshness to well-known portions of God's Word.

Tabhga

Descending some $2\frac{1}{2}$ miles Tabhga is reached. The church bearing witness to the multiplication of the loaves and fishes was rebuilt in 1982. It is simple but attractive and houses some beautiful mosaics of wild life as well as the 5th Century representation by the altar of a basket of loaves and fish.

Three of the gospels (e.g. John 6) record an exciting miracle performed in the hands of Jesus. Greek scholars tell us that the text is written in such a way that shows Jesus broke the loaves in one decisive action and as He **distributed** them, the act of multiplication occurred in His hands! A miracle at a point in history, yet speaking of a future breath-taking miracle – Calvary itself!

The time would come when Jesus would be taken to the cross and broken; one definite, final act never to be repeated. Yet that 'break', that death would result in countless blessings as believers through the ages committed themselves to receive Him as Saviour and Lord, the One who, having become the bearer of the world's sin-problem could give them Eternal Life.

St. Peter's Primacy

Near to Tabhga's church but on the Lakeside is the Chapel of St. Peter's Primacy, known also as the Lord's Table, for here is recalled the post-resurrection 'breakfast' appearance of Jesus to the disciples. Up to three years previously these men had used all their energy and expertise in fishing; then they had met Jesus and He told them He would make them fishers of men.

They had experienced His leadership and authority, witnessed His love and humility as well as His power over sin and sickness and death itself. They had been stricken with fear – and guilt! – as the horror and trauma of the crucifixion had unfolded before them, and then were both elated and bewildered at His resurrection appearances. They had returned to Galilee and, through impatience, frustration or uncertainty had decided to go fishing. As dawn broke on a fruitless night Jesus appeared on the beach and the disciples found themselves invited to share breakfast with Him!

Read the heart-rending account of Peter's restoration (John 21) as Jesus deals with his guilt-ridden conscience and clears his confused mind, bringing back order and purpose and ministry.

'Peter, do you love me more than these?' That word 'these' could have referred to the other disciples – Peter had so strongly proclaimed his loyalty and devotion just a few days earlier only to be found wanting when the real test came; yet the phrase is so written that 'these' could have meant the big haul of fish lying on the shore! Did Jesus perceive that, in desperation Peter was returning to his first love, that occupation he knew he could do, meeting the challenges of weather and competition in a consistent manner?

What of us? Do we love the Lord more than the dearest thing in our lives, that which motivates us to work and action employing God-given skills? Would we give up that well-paid job, that influential position in order to be obedient to His call? Not that these things are wrong in themselves for He can be glorified in the way we work and prosper.

Yet if He said, 'Come, this is now my chosen path for you; lay down your success and security, take up a new, unknown challenge' – would the call of the 'fish' outweigh the call of the Master?

Twice Jesus asks Peter, 'Do you love me?' using a word implying a sacrificial love that is given even when it is not reciprocated. Twice Peter defends his love for Jesus but uses a word denoting a great affection and high regard, yet falling short of the high commitment Jesus is seeking.

The third time, Jesus lowers His requirement and, using Peter's own term virtually says, 'Do you really have a great affection and high regard for me, Peter?' Peter is grieved as he realises he is falling short of what his Master requires. 'What you have said is true, Lord.'

The important thing is that Jesus takes Peter at the point where He is and commissions him to a loving, caring, teaching ministry, prophesying that his devotion to carrying out that commission would bring him into situations and places not of his own making nor choosing. The time was going to come when his 'great affection and high regard' would be transformed into a sacrificial love causing him to be completely dedicated no matter what the cost.

That's true for us also. Jesus always takes us just as He finds us, and provided we are willing to face up to the challenge He presents, will enable us to do His Will and, step by step will transform and strengthen us to become worthwhile members of His Kingdom.

✤ ✤ ✤

St. Peter's Primacy

'My child, I know your heart;
  I know your deepest thoughts;
I know your every longing,
  your strong points and your faults.
I ask that you be honest;
  I'll take you as you are;
I'll change you and I'll mould you,
  I'll take the things that mar,
I'm looking for devotion,
  the true and willing heart;
For single-minded purpose
  from which you'll not depart.
I'm looking for disciples
  who will tend and care and teach,
Will you be amongst that number?
  How many will you reach?'

✤ ✤ ✤

Capernaum

Capernaum is literally Kfar Nahum – village of Nahum. In the time of Jesus it was a busy and important frontier town on the Syrian border. There would have been a Roman garrison together with a customs control where Levi was the officiating tax officer.

The town became the centre of Jesus' Galilean ministry and there are incidents recorded like the healing of Peter's mother-in-law, the curing of the centurion's servant, the paying of tax and the casting out of evil spirits from the man in the synagogue.

Yet despite the wonder of miracles like these and the challenge that Jesus' ministry would have made, there must have been a prevailing hardness in the hearts of those townsfolk. It seems strange that this should have been so yet Jesus declared (Matthew 11:23) that if the miracles witnessed in Capernaum had been performed in Sodom, it would have remained to that present time! When we consider the rampant wickedness that caused Sodom's destruction, what was Capernaum really like? Jesus prophesied,

And you, Capernaum, will you be lifted up to the skies? No, you will go down to the depths.

(some translations prefer the word 'hell')

One hundred years later that prophecy was fulfilled!

The ruins of the synagogue seen today are probably of the one built upon the site where Jesus worshipped and taught. Nearby, excavations revealed the remains of 1st century houses one of which had been used as a 'home church' and believed to be St. Peter's; subsequently, a church was built over the site in the 5th century. Today's modern chapel was opened in 1991.

Despite the prevailing conditions in Capernaum, there were many people who **were** blessed and whose lives were changed because of the presence of Jesus in that town. Levi the Customs officer was such a one. He had probably seen, and no doubt heard Jesus speak on a number of occasions but never expected to hear Him say, 'Follow Me'. It was said in a tone that implied a command, not just an invitation – and the command was instantly obeyed. A literal translation of Jesus' words reads, 'Follow **with** me', and that brings fresh insight to an exciting situation.

Jesus isn't asking those who would follow Him to keep behind and copy exactly everything they see and hear; that is certainly challenging – and sometimes frustrating. Rather, He's inviting a side-by-side walk with Him, His strong but tender arm of love around each disciple, guiding, directing and leading each step that is taken. If you want a visual aid of such a situation consider these words of Jesus:

> *Come to me, all you who are weary and burdened, and I will give you rest. Take my yoke upon you and learn from me, for I am gentle and humble in heart, and you will find rest for your souls. For my yoke is easy and my burden is light.* (Matthew 11:28–30)

In those days it was a common sight to see two oxen yoked together working in the field. Sometimes one of the animals would be young and inexperienced not knowing when to go, when to stop or what to do; but it didn't matter because the other animal was experienced and knew everything. It had been well-trained and its every movement was automatically carried out by its young companion because they were yoked together in such a way that there was nothing else it could do but obey! That's like us and Jesus. He invites us to be joined to Him by a yoke of love that will make following with Him a fulfilling and exciting adventure!

Northern Galilee

Migdal

'*Migdal*' is the Hebrew word for 'tower' and archaeologists have discovered remains of columns that probably formed part of one or several towers. It is the site of Magdala and the traditional home of Mary Magdalene. Josephus, the Jewish general and famed historian, made the town his headquarters and at that time there were several thousand inhabitants with a large fleet of boats. The town was destroyed by the Romans under Vespasian and Titus.

Safed

Safed is the most northerly city in Israel and at 2800 feet above sea level is the highest. It is one of the four holy cities for Jews, the others being Jerusalem, Hebron and Tiberias. Fortified by Josephus, Safed rebelled against the Romans in AD 66 and following the destruction of the Temple four years later many of the priestly families moved here together with those wishing to study the Torah.

However, it was as a result of the Jews being expelled from Spain (1492) and Portugal (1496) that many of them settled here causing Safed to become the City of Mysticism, a centre of learning and especially of the Zohar, the standard work of the Kabbala; this is a system of mysticism in which Kabbalists read hidden meanings into the Old Testament. The first Hebrew book was printed here in 1578.

In 1883 the Druze (which see) destroyed the town; also it experienced bitter fighting in 1948 but is now predominantly Jewish and a haven for Israeli artists.

Rosh Pinna

Established in 1882 on deserted rocky land this was the first settlement in Galilee. Its name was chosen from Psalm 118, *'The stone which the builders rejected is become the chief cornerstone'* or the head (Rosh) of the corner.

Hatzor

In biblical times, Hatzor was a city of strategic importance. In Joshua's day it was a chief stronghold of the Canaanites and the largest city in the Holy Land (Joshua 11:10). Joshua captured it; Solomon rebuilt it; and the Assyrians destroyed it in 732 BC. Under Professor Yigael Yadin's leadership excavations brought to light evidence of 22 separate cities. Most revealing is the water shaft; King Ahab's engineers had to dig down 38 metres in order to tap the natural ground water reservoir.

Dan

Once the most northerly town in Israel's Promised Land. Following Solomon's death the kingdom divided under Rehoboam in the south (two tribes) and Jeroboam in the north (ten tribes). The latter led the people into idolatrous worship and in order to dissuade them from attending Temple Services in Jerusalem he cast two golden calves proclaiming them to be Israel's gods! One was set up in Bethel and the other at Dan.

Baneas – Caesarea Philippi

A few minutes drive from Dan is the majestic power of the Baneas waterfall. Collecting water from the melting snows of Mt Hermon this rushing, turbulent splendour is a major contributor to the River Jordan.

Just over a mile to the east is Baneas proper – the Arabic rendering for the Greek *'Paneas'*. At one time a shrine for Baal was erected here and later the Greeks worshipped Pan the god of shepherds, and niches devoted to this purpose are still to be seen in the cliff face.

Caesar Augustus presented the district to Herod the Great who erected and dedicated a temple to the Emperor near to the spring. On Herod's death it passed to his youngest son Philip who established Baneas as his capital re-naming it Caesarea Philippi thus distinguishing it from Caesarea on the Mediterranean coast.

The Bible records a time when Jesus and the disciples visited the area and, possibly because of the evidence of pagan shrines and worship Jesus posed the ultimate question everyone has to answer at some time in their life. *'Who do people say the Son of Man is?'* (Matthew 16:13). After a variety of answers Peter blurts out, *'You are the Christ* (the Messiah), *the Son of the living God.'*

It would be good to pause here a while in this most attractive area with its different levels of water and consider our own answer to the same question.

'Who do People Say That I, the Son of Man, am?'

Some said a Prophet, Teacher,
Great Leader, Earthly King,
Messiah – or Imposter!
In fact 'most anything;

   Some said I was the Saviour,
   Come down from heaven above,
   They said I was the Father's Son,
   His gift of endless love;

Yet through the ages they've debated,
Argued, struggled, fought,
Concerning who they said I was,
Concerning what they thought;

   Through trauma, persecution, murder,
   Just to have their way,
   So rarely did they listen
   To what I had to say!

I am the Lord, the Holy One; in flesh I came to save
My own creation from the grip of sin's eternal grave.

Yet force I never countenanced to bring about
      salvation,
I gave man free-will to choose, without such
      provocation,
If force there be, then it is **love** – the most compelling
      kind,
The love that seeks to find the lost, an endless search
      to find
a people who'll return my love – pure, true and
      without sham;
Are you amongst that number; who do **you** say that I
      am?'

The Golan Heights

The Golan is the name of a mountainous range of volcanic formation rising on the eastern shore of the Sea of Galilee and running northwards along the Upper Jordan as far as the Hermon range. The Heights of the Golan are actually in the land of Jordan about 4000 feet above sea level and stretching into Syria.

According to Scripture and history the Golan is an integral part of Israel, being a portion of the inheritance of the half-tribe of Manasseh. The actual town of Golan was one of the Old Testament cities of Refuge.

At the end of World War I the Golan area was attached to Syria under the French Mandate. When Syria was defeated by Israel in the War of Independence (1948), the Syrians fortified themselves on the Golan Heights and were able to bring Galilee under constant attack. At the outbreak of the Six Days' War (1967) and in response to Syria's heavy bombardment the Israeli army ousted the Syrians in order to bring peace to northern Galilee.

Leaving Banias the road climbs, passing through the Druze village of Mas'ada which lies to the east of Majdal-Shams (Tower of the Sun) the chief Druze town in the area.

Bereikhat Ram (Height Pool)

Bereikhat Ram is about seven miles beyond Banias and is said by some to be the crater of an extinct volcano containing a natural pool. Up to 30 feet in depth, the water is good for swimming with a low salt content. A delightful spot when the roses are in bloom from which to view the slopes of Hermon.

Gamla

A vastly impressive natural fortress rising from a valley and linked to a plateau by a narrow ridge of land. Thousands of Jews from the Golan sought refuge here when the Roman General Vespasian besieged the site in AD 67. Despite initial success against the Romans the final battle saw several thousand Jews slaughtered whilst a further 5000 committed suicide by throwing themselves over the cliff.

Kursi

The traditional 'land of the Gadarenes' where Jesus cast out many demons from the demented man Legion and gave them permission to enter into a herd of pigs which subsequently drowned (Mark 5:1). It was one of the 10 cities of the Decapolis, a league formed for trade and mutual defence around AD 1 contained in a large area mainly to the south of Galilee and east of the Jordan River although it included Beth Shean to the west and Damascus in the north.

The remains of a nearby ancient harbour were accidentally discovered during road construction in the late 1960s. A fifth-century monastery with some beautiful mosaic floors was excavated in 1970. For some unknown reason the area was abandoned in the 8th century. The site is now a National Park.

Susita

About 1000 feet above the Sea of Galilee are the ruins of the Greek city Hippos, another of the Decapolis with remains of five churches and a large water system that brought water from the Golan Heights. A Jewish community existed here in the 2nd/3rd centuries AD. Susita is derived from a Hebrew word for 'horse' – Hippos is the Greek equivalent; some think the contour of the land suggests a horse's back.

Ein Gev

This kibbutz, established in 1937 from a sandy strip of land is now an attractive development famous for its fish restaurant, fish canning, and its fleet of motor boats. Also, its concert hall housing many events including the annual Ein Gev Music Festival held during Passover.

The well-known St. Peter's fish (so named as tradition holds it was one of this family that held in its mouth the coin required by Jesus to pay tax – Matthew 17:27) belong to the Cichlid family and can weigh up to $4\frac{1}{2}$ lbs with a length of 15 feet. The adults keep their young in their mouths until they can move around independently.

In 1939 the Kibbutz Nir David (just west of Beit She'an), invested some money in a fish farm which many folk thought quite imprudent. Although St. Peter fish are grey-black in colour the kibbutz have managed by a process of developing natural mutations to produce a red strain which has a firmer flesh and lower fat content.

Hamat Gader

This is the site of the famous hot springs. The remains of a Roman theatre, temple and bath houses can be seen – plus a modern alligator farm!

The Druze

The Druze (whose traditional ancestor is Jethro, Moses' father-in-law) live in a score of villages in Galilee as well as on the slopes of Mt Hermon, southern Syria and south Lebanon.

Originating in Egypt around AD 1000, the Druze were an heretical sect from Islam under a Muslim missionary named Darazi from whom they get their name. With their mixture of biblical and koranic teaching they revere one God and believe in reincarnation. They are a closed community divided into 'the wise' and 'the ignorant'.

The 'wise' are initiated into the secret doctrines of the community and any adult Druze can ask for initiation which is a severe test – it is believed that failures have another chance in their next life. The 'wise' wear a distinguishing garment and white turban; they share in Thursday religious services, lead daily prayer, and abstain from alcohol, lying, theft and revenge.

The Druze are very adept at forecasting each winter's severity. Every year on 26 September the village Elders from Majdal-Shams, Mas'ada and Bukata perform a test with sprinkled salt on a plate. It is left on a roof overnight and if dry in the morning the winter will be dry. Partially dissolved salt indicates a moderate winter whilst salt that is completely dissolved speaks of a very cold, wet and snowy winter. They serve visitors a winter treat of grape-juice poured over a bowl of snow which they say heats the body and cleanses the blood.

The Final Hours

The Upper Room

Each person must decide for themselves whether the Syrian Church of St. Mark located in the Armenian Quarter of the Old City or the Cenacle on Mount Zion is the site of the Upper Room of the gospels where Jesus kept His last Passover meal. In discussing the various traditions it is easy to overlook the actual significance of the meal itself and how it came about and so we discuss it in Part IV under the heading 'Passover, Seder and the Lord's Supper'.

Gethsemane

We shall never understand nor comprehend the agony and trauma witnessed by this place. Jesus comes to spend His final hours of freedom in communion with His Father. His humanity desperately yearns for some other answer than the Cross, but immediately He comes against such thoughts and desires, confessing He only wants to keep in line with Father's Will. He is so overwhelmed by the horror of becoming sin and the tension is so great that His sweat becomes great drops of blood, all part of the intense suffering that took Him to Pilate's scourging and finally the Cross itself.

Yet Jesus, in the power of the Spirit manifested complete control the whole time. John in his gospel (chapter 18) preserves an incident which illustrates this fact in a startling but convincing way. The soldiers come to arrest Jesus; He asks whom they are seeking. 'Jesus of Nazareth' they reply. Jesus answers, 'I AM' – the name of God Himself, the

'I AM THAT I AM' God who led the Israelites out of Egypt – and the effect on the soldiers is supernatural! They fall backwards and are powerless to do anything; they are paralysed by the power of God! Until released by Jesus they are as good as dead. They aren't able to arrest Jesus by force – rather He gives Himself into their hands. He is in control all the time!

Gethsemane

Gethsemane, the olive grove of quietness and serenity; of times spent in communion with Father and with friends; it becomes the place of sorrow, of anguish and of agony, in facing all the horror of impending death – for others!

The Sinless One, the Perfect One who never erred from doing all that Father had decreed should come to pass. Facing the horrific reality of becoming sin for man; perhaps sensing how abhorrent He would become in the eyes of Father God.

Did He realise that fellowship between the two of them would be broken for a time?
How could He picture going into the abyss of hell?

Yet He knew He would gain the victory, He knew the triumph would be His because we read in Luke 9:51,

> *'As the time approached for him **to be taken up to heaven** Jesus resolutely set out for Jerusalem.'*

Already He was looking beyond the trial, His death and burial, even His resurrection. He was anticipating the thrill of victory, of triumph over evil, the conquest of Satan and the fulfilment of Father's Will. The final battle was won in Gethsemane as Jesus declared 'Not my Will but yours be done.'

✣ ✣ ✣

The Trial(s) of Jesus

It is obvious that this time of Jesus being subjected to ridicule, abuse and hypocritical accusation was a complete travesty of justice. The Sanhedrin were guilty of serious misconduct.

For example, their function was to protect and be on the side of any accused person brought before them; but here they were plotting to kill the accused!

Under Jewish Law witnesses had to commence proceedings against the accused; here it was the Sanhedrin who did so and were at a loss to find any witnesses!

The Law forbade capital cases to be tried at night – but Jesus was!

Judgements by the Sanhedrin had to be delayed until the following day, and even then could not be heard if that day was the eve of a Sabbath or Festival – yet the Sanhedrin overruled these and other legal requirements in their intense desire to be rid of Jesus!

It is not easy to achieve complete agreement on the sequence of events in the last earthly hours of Jesus but in dove-tailing the various gospel accounts the pattern could have been similar to the following:

- Jesus is taken before Annas (John 18:12–24)
- He is then taken before Caiaphas and the Sanhedrin (Matthew 26:57; Mark 14:53)
- Second meeting of the Sanhedrin (Luke 22:66; Mark 15:1)
- Jesus is taken before Pilate (Matthew 27:11; Luke 23:2; John 18:28)
- He is then taken to Herod (Luke 23:6–12)
- He is returned to Pilate (Matthew 27:11–26; Mark 15:1–15)
- Barabbas is released; Jesus is scourged (Luke 23:13–25; John 19:1–16)
- He is crucified (John 19:17–30)

St. Peter in Gallicantu (The Church of the Cock-Crowing)

Built on the traditional site of the house or palace of Caiaphas the church presents a powerful visual aid to the gospel record. Due to the steepness of the hill-side the building is on four levels.

Beneath today's church on the second level was the courtyard where one can imagine Peter warming himself by the open fire – and denying all knowledge of the Man he had so recently declared to be the Son of God!

Descending to the third level the visitor enters the stark reality of an ancient guardroom complete with two pillars between which prisoners would have been tied and mercilessly flogged with the deadly scourge. This is not where Jesus received such punishment but could certainly be where the apostles were flogged after the Resurrection for refusing to stop preaching the good news of Jesus (Acts 5:40, 41).

At the lowest level is the condemned cell reached today by a flight of stone steps from the guardroom although in Jesus' time there was no such entrance. Condemned prisoners would have been lowered through the 'neck' of this foul-smelling, bottle-like prison and subsequently removed the same way.

Is this cell, once dark, damp, perhaps rat-infested the humiliating place where the Son of God waited, possibly for some long time before the Sanhedrin were able to continue the wicked work started during the early night hours?

Jesus had won the battle in Gethsemane where He determined to do His Father's Will and drink the very last dregs of the terrifying cup of the Cross. The hours spent in isolation would have been traumatic to endure; the angels would certainly have continued their ministry to Him and the many Scriptures He had memorised would have been a great source of strength and comfort. But His humanity would have agonised in silence waiting for the dawn.

Ecce Homo ('Behold the Man') *Convent*

The Convent, belonging to the Sisters of Zion marks the second of the 14 Stations of the Cross (which see under **Via**

Dolorosa) and adds considerable meaning to the Scriptures
concerning the mocking of Jesus by the soldiers. This is
thought to be the location of the Antonia Fortress guarding
the north-east corner of the city wall which also gave
the military excellent control over the Temple area in the
event of riots or similar disturbances.

Beneath the Convent, excavations have revealed what
until recently was believed to be the Pavement (see John
19:13) where Pilate gave judgement against Jesus. In this
area, games played by off-duty soldiers were etched on the
Roman paving slabs including one known as 'the Game of
the King' which can be seen.

Precise details are not clear but it seems a condemned
prisoner would be taken, dressed as a burlesque king and
paid mock homage which developed into general ill-
treatment. This certainly gives added meaning to the
gospel account (Mark 15:16–20).

Ecce Homo Convent

Is this the place, dear Saviour
You were scourged, derided, mocked?
The lashes tearing at your flesh,
Your frame completely shocked!
You'd triumphed over anguish in dark Gethsemane,
You heard the dread word 'crucify';
It had to be the tree!

No matter where the place was,
No matter where You stood,
The truth is that you suffered –
You plainly understood
The last stage was unfolding,
In stark reality,
You knew the road must end upon the Cross –
at Calvary!

Yet deep inside (we know not how) You had abiding
peace,

You were fulfilling Father's Will to bring mankind
     release from Satan's kingdom – darkness! all evil,
     sin and spite;
To break his grip forever! To bring us into Light!
As members of Your family, adopted just like sons,
To act with Your authority, Your own, Your chosen
     ones!

Dear Jesus, may your Spirit have full access every day
     to minister in and through us, that You will have
     Your way to build up lives and strengthen; equip,
     direct and use,
Each day please make us willing, in any way You
     choose!

✣ ✣ ✣

The Flagellation

Adjacent to, and before reaching the Ecce Homo Convent
is the Franciscan Convent of the Flagellation; its two
chapels memorialise the Scourging and Condemnation of
Jesus. Pause a while and let the horror of this appalling
punishment cause you to be amazed at the depth of God's
love for you.

The scourge, in the hands of a skilful flogger could cause
excruciating pain and agony. Composed of leather thongs
in which pieces of bone or metal were embedded, the
torturer could rip and tear the flesh even to the exposing
of the victim's bone!

The prophet Isaiah (chapter 53) writing some 750 years
before the event, not only alludes to crucifixion (unknown
in his day) but also to scourging. Verse 4 of this chapter
reads,

Surely he took up our infirmities and carried our sorrows.

That word 'infirmities' comes from the Hebrew 'to be
weak, sick or afflicted'. Verse 5 says,

> *He was pierced for our transgressions,*
> *He was crushed for our iniquities,*
> *The punishment that brought us peace was upon him*
> *and by his wounds we are healed.*

The word 'healed' more literally means 'made whole, normal'.

Are you able to believe that in His horrible, dreadful scourging Jesus was taking upon Himself in some miraculous way our sicknesses, our illnesses, our weaknesses and our infirmities? It seems fantastic, but that's what Scripture says!

We must never lose sight of the fact that the biggest miracle is that those who are spiritually dead to God can be made alive in Him by a simple faith and trust in the death and resurrection of Jesus. Yet we were created as whole beings and He desires the very best for our bodies, minds and emotions as well as our spirits. In providing us with salvation God has made provision for our wholeness – are we able to take such a big step of faith?

The Via Dolorosa
(The Way of Pain – the Stations of the Cross)

Those travelling the Via Dolorosa in a group will be adequately catered for by their leader so the following is written with individuals primarily in mind. Although we don't know the exact route along which Jesus was taken to the Cross, the fourteen Stations which are incidents in His last agonising walk encourage us to pray and meditate upon these events. Nine of them are taken from the gospels and the remainder from legend.

1st Station – Jesus is condemned to death
This is located in the playground of the Al-Omariya Moslem school and when open the entrance is reached via a ramp. Once thought to be part of the Antonia Fortress the windows of the school look out onto the Temple area that it guarded (Mark 15:1–15).

2nd Station – Jesus receives His Cross
This is remembered outside the Chapel of the Condemnation (John 19:13–17).

3rd Station – Jesus falls for the first time
Proceeding under the Ecce Homo arch to the end of the road this Station is commemorated round to the left outside the Polish chapel served by Armenian Catholics (Isaiah 53:4). Notice the roadway; when it was built up some Roman paving stones were used.

4th Station – Jesus meets His Mother
A few steps farther on is a plaque above a chapel door bringing this incident to remembrance (Luke 2:34–5).

5th Station – Simon helps Jesus carry the Cross
A short way past the 4th Station the Via Dolorosa turns right and uphill. On the left-hand corner an inscription over the door of a Roman Catholic chapel tells that the cross was laid on Simon of Cyrene. The road we have just left leads in from Damascus Gate; is that how Simon came to be there (Mark 15:21)?

6th Station – Veronica wipes the face of Jesus
Halfway up the stepped street on the left-hand side a Crusader vaulted room has been turned into a simple chapel which is served by the 'Little Sisters of Jesus' founded by Charles de Foucauld. The legend behind this Station is that a woman wiped the face of Jesus with her headscarf which retained a permanent imprint of His face (Veronica means 'true likeness') (Isaiah 53:1–3).

7th Station – Jesus falls the second time
At the top of the street is the junction with the busy north-south market and directly opposite beside a pillar which was once part of a colonnade lining the street the Station is marked.

8th Station – Jesus speaks to the daughters of Jerusalem
Just to the left of the 7th Station pillar, the east-west road we were on continues uphill. A short way along on the left

(opposite the shops) is a small cross set in a high wall bearing the words IC XC NIKA – Jesus Christ conquers (Luke 23:27–31).

9th Station – Jesus falls the third time
From the 8th Station it is necessary to return to the junction and this time turn right through the market for about 60 yards. On the right is a stone stairway leading to a terrace containing little dwellings where Abyssinian monks live; the entrance marks the Station.

10th Station – Jesus is stripped of His garments
The remaining five Stations are all observed within the Church of the Holy Sepulchre. From the 9th Station it is possible to descend through the Coptic Chapel which is worth a visit, or to return to the market thoroughfare and continue to the next turning on the right; both routes will lead to the Church courtyard. The 10th Station is observed inside the main door to the right at the foot of the steps leading to Calvary or upstairs with the 11th Station (Luke 19:23, 24).

11th Station – Jesus nailed to the Cross
At the top of the steps are two chapels. The one on the right belongs to the Roman Catholics where this traumatic event is remembered (Luke 23:33–43).

12th Station – Jesus dies on the Cross
The chapel on the left which belongs to the Greek Orthodox records the death of Jesus. Under the altar is a hole where it is possible to touch the rock traditionally thought to be where the Cross was set (John 19:28–30).

13th Station – Jesus taken down from the Cross
Descending from Calvary the Stone of Anointing marks the spot where it is said Jesus' body rested prior to burial (Psalm 22:14, 15).

14th Station – Jesus is laid in the Sepulchre
The tomb is in the centre of the church and is entered through the 'watching chamber' (Matthew 27:59, 60).

The Garden Tomb

From the 4th century the Church of the Holy Sepulchre has been recognised by the major churches as marking the site of Calvary and the tomb of Jesus. Many books describe the Church and some go into the argument for and against its authenticity so there is no need to attempt that now. Nor is there any intention to take from that place any blessing that visitors and pilgrims have derived from its existence. However, much more deserves to be said of the Garden Tomb than most books allow.

It was about 150 years ago that some archaeologists started to question the traditional site of Golgotha (Place of the Skull) believing it to be located to the north of the Old City. Of course, there is endless discussion concerning where the City walls were in the time of Jesus; however, records show that the lower courses of the present wall stretching eastwards from Damascus Gate to Herod's Gate are definitely Herodian and so would appear to be a part of the city's northern wall in the time of Jesus.

Standing in the Garden on the stone platform at Skull Hill you are faced with a rather noisy bus station! Yet if you could have stood here about 3000 years ago you would have been standing on the northern slopes of Mount Moriah. This elevation stretched southwards to the Temple area where the Dome of the Rock now stands.

Moriah figures in biblical sacrifice for it was here that God tested Abraham's love and loyalty in the matter of Isaac, and here that Solomon built the magnificent Temple to his God. Where did he obtain those great slabs of stone that had to be cut to shape and 'dressed' to the last detail before being transported to the site?

To the east of Damascus Gate is an entrance to Solomon's Quarries revealing a vast area stretching a long way under the city that has been heavily quarried. It seems highly probable that in addition to this, the large space now taken up by the bus station was the result of extensive quarrying of Moriah's northern slopes providing the many tons of stone the Temple required.

When the available stone was removed, a spent quarry remained and later Jewish tradition associated this site with their 'Beit-ha-Sekilah' – the Place of Stoning. In early Christian times the northern entrance to the city was known as St. Stephen's Gate – was this in memory of the first Christian martyr who maybe met his death at this Place of Stoning?

Whilst stoning was the throwing of stones at the accused, we are told the Jewish Talmud also reveals the opposite – that the body was sometimes thrown at the stones! The victim would be taken to the top of Moriah (today's Skull Hill where there is a Moslem cemetery) and thrown off! If the fall didn't kill him one of his accusers would be ready with stones to complete the punishment. Whilst such a death was horrific, crucifixion was much worse!

The Romans, who ruled the country at the time of Jesus always chose an open space near a highway to crucify their victims; this was to ensure that the terrible agony and torture of such a death would be seen by a great many people and serve as a strong deterrent to other potential law-breakers.

The gospels record that there were those 'passing by' as Jesus hung on the Cross (Matthew 27:39). This worked-out quarry would have served the Romans ideally as it was bordered on its northern side by the road running to Jericho whilst the main road to Damascus skirted its western side.

The skull-like effect on Moriah's north cliff face may or may not have added to the assumption that this was Golgotha; it certainly impressed the British General Gordon (of Khartoum fame) who in 1883 spent some leave in Israel doing biblical research.

However, if this **is** the place of crucifixion then there should be evidence of a 1st Century garden nearby containing a tomb cut from solid rock (Matthew 27:60). We know

Joseph of Arimathea was a rich man (Matthew 27:57) and perhaps he owned the garden as well as the tomb?

Excavations on the site have revealed several cisterns, the largest having a capacity of no less than 200,000 gallons! Dating before the Christian era it is hewn out of solid rock and the cost of such an excavation not only suggests an owner of wealth but an extensive growing area that demanded such a volume of water to support it. The discovery nearby in 1924 of a very fine 1st century wine-press is evidence of the area having included a vineyard – perhaps at the time of Jesus?

Whilst archaeology can always bring divergence of opinion there are experts who maintain that the tomb in the Garden is of 1st Century origin; its unusual height and the fact that half its interior is designed just as a weeping chamber points to a wealthy owner. Also, it is possible to view the burial place from outside the tomb (John 20:5).

The various bits of the jig-saw certainly seem to fit together in this location which today covers about an acre of land and abounds with trees, plants, flowers and herbs of many different varieties. It is an oasis of peace and tranquillity despite the adjacent bus station and the restless activity of the Old City – and it is a paradise for the vast number of birds that nest and lodge in its security.

Of supreme importance, of course, is not so much **where** these amazing events happened but that they **did** take place! Jesus **was** crucified and in some miraculous way as He hung on the Cross God poured on Him the sin of the world making it possible for those who dare to believe to know forgiveness of sin.

Jesus **did** rise again on the third day and in so doing proved He had not only paid the penalty for the sin of the world but in defeating Satan at every level made the gift of Eternal Life available to all who will exercise faith and accept Him as Saviour and Lord.

For some that is a small step to take but for others a very big one. Scripture comes alive in this garden in a unique

way and it is certainly an ideal place to meditate upon that
which can dramatically change a life for all time!

✣ ✣ ✣

The Garden Tomb, so full of trees and shrubs and
plants and flowers,
A haven 'midst the bustle, noise and busyness, of
hours
of pilgrimage, of visiting, of churches, sites – and
talking!
With mixed emotions, joy – and weariness from
endless walking!
To sit and pray, to meditate and think upon the Lord,
To visualise the graphic scenes portrayed within His
Word.

As morning light wakes up the Garden, birds in
chorus sing
A glorious anthem full of praise for every living thing.
Was this the place one early morn God's power was
displayed?
When Jesus broke the bonds of death and from the
Tomb was raised?
His friends had not expected such a miracle could be,
They hadn't understood the Scripture in reality.
He'd told them time and time again what He must
undergo,
The trial, scourging, cruel death – they didn't want to
know!
Yet Jesus fulfilled everything, it happened as He said,
He won the victory on the Cross and now, raised
from the dead
Their amazement turns to wonder and their wonder
turns to praise,
With Him they're reunited; now others they'll amaze
with all the truth of Calvary; their work will never
cease
Till all the world embraces the great news of God's
release.

So as you pause to meditate be open to His voice,
Be sure of **your** Eternity, be sure you can rejoice
in knowing God's forgiveness, of being covered by His
    grace,
Restored into His family! Held by His love's embrace.

The Garden Tomb – Jerusalem

A glimpse of the Sea of Galilee

Storm-tossed Sea of Galilee

The Golden Gate viewed from the Garden of Gethsemane

View of the Dome of the Rock (the Temple Site) from the Al'Omariya College
(1st Station of the Cross)

*Bronze Menorah standing opposite the entrance to the Knessett.
A gift of friendship from the UK.*

Celebrating Bar Mitzvah at the Western Wall

The Citadel – David's Tower by the Jaffa Gate

Windmill erected by Sir Moses Montefiore (at Yemin Moshe)
founder of New Jerusalem

PART II

Some Customs and Symbols

Some Customs and Symbols

Bar Mitzvah

this means 'Son of the Commandment' and is applied to
Jewish boys on reaching the age of 13; they are then said
to be mature having reached manhood and are obliged to
accept the teachings of the Law. In many Orthodox
congregations boys have to pass an examination in Hebrew
and the basics of the Jewish religion before becoming Bar
Mitzvah which is then officially recognised at the first
public reading of the Torah after his 13th birthday.

For the last 70 years a Bat Mitzvah ceremony has been
held for Jewish girls, usually around the age of 12 as they
are considered to mature earlier than boys. The essence of
these ceremonies is the call to the candidate to recite the
blessings over the Torah.

Circumcision

The Hebrew word for circumcision is *'brit'* which means
'covenant'. God entered into a Covenant with Abraham
(Genesis 17) whereby He promised to give the land of
Canaan as an everlasting possession to Abraham and all his
descendants through Isaac who was yet to be born. Ishmael
would also be blessed and become the father of twelve
rulers but God emphasised the Covenant would be established in Isaac.

The sign of the Covenant is the act of circumcision
which is usually performed on the eighth day following a
boy's birth; it is considered to be the most important of all
the commandments.

In Exodus 13:1, 2 God commanded every first-born
male to be consecrated to Him; to avoid his life being
dedicated to the service of God it was necessary for the boy
to be redeemed. This 'Redemption of the First-born Son'
Ceremony is carried out today on the 31st day after the
birth by payment of a sum of money to the priest.

Menorah

The seven-branched candelabrum was the centrepiece of the Tabernacle and subsequently of the Temple. It is very much a Jewish symbol and when Israel declared Independence in 1948 Britain presented the new State with a bronze Menorah measuring 15 × 12 feet. Panels on the branches depict figures and events in Jewish history. It is erected across the street from the Knesset (Parliament).

Mezuzah

The word *'Mezuzah'* (plural *'mezuzot'*) in Hebrew means 'doorpost'. It is the name given to a small receptacle and the roll of parchment it contains. The roll bears the following hand-written words from Deuteronomy 6:4–9,

> *Hear, O Israel: The Lord our God, the Lord is one. Love the Lord your God with all your heart and with all your soul and with all your strength. These commandments that I give you today are to be upon your hearts. Impress them upon your children. Talk about them when you sit at home and when you walk along the road, when you lie down and when you get up. Tie them as symbols on your hands and bind them on your foreheads. Write them on the door-frames of your houses and on your gates.*

The passage is known as *'Shema'*, Hebrew for its first word 'Hear'. Mezuzot are placed at eye level on the righthand doorpost of the house and outside most of its rooms. As a gesture of reverence, Jews on entering a home will touch the mezuzah with their fingertips, kissing them and saying, 'May God protect my going out and coming in, now and forever'.

Phylacteries *(Tefilin)*

The fixing of mezuzot as well as the wearing of phylacteries arises out of the above commandment. Whilst many commentators maintain the instruction was meant metaphorically, phylacteries were in evidence by the time of Jesus and a universal custom by the 2nd century AD.

Orthodox Jews use them in a highly devotional way putting them on in a set pattern accompanied by meditative prayer. The phylactery is a small leather cube up to $1\frac{1}{2}$ inches square, the one for the head having four compartments but the one for the arm having no divisions. The former contains four passages of Scripture on separate strips of parchment, whilst the latter has the same verses on a single strip. They are Exodus 13:1–10 and 11–16, Deuteronomy 6:4–9 and 11:13–21.

Phylacteries are fastened by black straps, the one around the head between the eyebrows and level with the hair line, the other on the (usually) left arm close to the elbow with the straps wound seven times around the arm towards the hand and round the fingers in a designated pattern.

The one on the arm is a reminder of God's outstretched arm in protecting the Jewish people from evil and signifies His relationship to Israel; the one on the head indicates the duty of subjecting the longings and desires of the heart to God's service and symbolises Israel's relationship to the Lord.

The Prayer Shawl (Tallit) and Fringes (tziziot)

Numbers 15:37–41 records the words of the Lord to Moses that the people should make fringes (tassels) on the corners of their garments, each fringe bearing a blue cord. They were to be a reminder of God's commandments and the Prayer Shawl was designed to carry them. They are twisted and knotted in a traditional manner although the 2nd century rabbis agreed that the blue cord could be dispensed with; because of this the embroidery on many shawls is blue.

Shabbat

Jewish days begin at nightfall and extend for 24 hours. *Shabbat*, the Jewish Sabbath commences Friday night and in order not to desecrate it by miscalculating the time when night actually falls it is customary for candles (an expression of light and joy) to be lit at sundown, about 18 minutes before sunset and some forty minutes before nightfall. Since Bible times the Sabbath has been central in Jewish life when families meet to eat, pray, study and sing together.

Swaying

Jewish people are quite distinctive in adopting a swaying or rocking motion when praying although its origin seems unclear. A second-century Rabbi suggested that the spirit of man was the lamp of the Lord referred to in Proverbs 20:27 and as such 'flickered' in harmony with the Torah. A different reason stems from the time before printed books were available.

Where a group had to share one book it would be placed on the ground and each person taking it in turns would continuously move forward, bend to read and then move backwards again producing a swaying movement. Others would say that it is just an expression of the rhythm of the prayer.

Synagogue

Following the destruction of the first Temple in 586 BC which was the central place of sacrifice and worship, synagogues were established in certain areas. They were essentially places of prayer to begin with but over the years their function changed. They became community meeting halls known as the Bet Knesset – House of Assembly – and when they became places for study they acquired the name Bet Midrash – House of Study.

Talmud

Consisting of a vast collection of information and instruction explaining the teachings of the Bible the Talmud covers virtually every area of human life and interest.

The first part is called the *Mishna* containing the teachings of scholars stretching over 1000 years from the time of Ezra, and is the authoritative source of Jewish Law. The second part, which is a commentary on the Mishna is called the *Gemara*.

Tanach

This is the name sometimes given to the Bible and is an acronym from the Hebrew words for its three parts:
– *Torah* – the Law, the five books of Moses – the Pentateuch;
– *Nevim* – the Prophets;
– *Ketuvim* – the Holy Writings.
TNK with vowels added gives the word 'Tanach', sometimes transliterated as 'Tanak'.

Yarmulke

'Yarmulke' is Yiddish and 'Kippah' is Hebrew for 'skullcap'. Some Jews maintain that covering the head is associated with showing reverence for God although biblically it was only the High Priest who was required to wear headgear and then only when performing his priestly duties. Despite there being no Scriptural basis for wearing a kippah, observant Jews wear one all the time. Some Jews do so when they are praying, studying or at mealtimes whilst others never do.

Many Christians point to 1 Corinthians 11:4 with the teaching that a man's head should not be covered when praying or prophesying. However, the Jewish New Testament Commentary points out that the literal translation of the verse is 'Every man who prays or prophesies **wearing something down over his head** brings shame to his head...' and that Paul is referring to wearing a veil and not a hat.

PART III

Six Biblical Trees

The Jewish National Fund is responsible for a team of several hundred engaged in planting and maintaining about a million acres of forest.

Many, many millions of trees have been planted, radically altering the face of the Land and its fertility as well as the climactic conditions.

Following the heavy snowstorms in January 1992, said to be the heaviest in living memory, a professor at the Hebrew University stated that half the Jerusalem trees were unable to cope with such a fall, the magnitude of which seems likely to occur every 10 years or so.

Some trees were planted because of their quick growth but as this produces weak wood they are unable to withstand such an attack. Trees that are flexible, like the cedar of Lebanon, are ideal because their branches bend under the snow until the weight is dislodged allowing their branches to regain their normal position.

In 1998 Israel's 50th Anniversary 'Year of Jubileé', the Festival of Tu B'shvat (often called the New Year for Trees) was celebrated with the planting of 500,000 trees all over the country.

The Olive Tree Speaks of Usefulness

Extremely beneficial in itself as well as in the fruit it yields the olive tree loves the sun and, although slow growing it lives to an exceptional age; in fact it never really dies! When cut down, the stump and roots will produce new shoots and eventually bear more fruit.

Although history records that the Romans cut down all available trees for mass crucifixions when they besieged Jerusalem, it is quite probable that the olive trees in the Garden of Gethsemane are the 'children' of those in Jesus' time.

It is said the tree's gnarled trunk speaks of Israel's tortuous history; its green leaf proclaims prosperity (Psalm 52:8) and its silver underside redemption. The wood is hard, durable and beautiful with a most distinctive contrasting grain.

The fruit must be harvested before the first rains of winter begin although the time for doing so is quite critical; a week before the olives are ready they wont drop. Sometimes the trees are shaken, or beaten with sticks causing the fruit to fall to the ground; some trees are climbed and the olives picked in a more usual manner.

Some are pickled to be used during the next twelve months whilst the rest is for producing oil – it is known for a full-grown tree in a good year to yield half a ton of oil! Just think of the many uses oil has.

It is basic to cooking and eating and a valuable source of light. Important for anointing and medicinal purposes, it is also used in cosmetics, soap-making and for lubrication.

How useful are we? The oil is the result of the fruit being washed, crushed and treated to produce pure oil. All born-again believers have been washed in the blood of Jesus, but are we prepared to be disciplined of the Lord, to undergo a crushing experience in order for Him to produce in us something that is really worthwhile?

It's a sobering thought that if we submit to His 'breaking and moulding' our usefulness will be increased immeasurably.

The Fig Tree Warns of Hypocrisy

In Mark 11:12–14 we read of an incident that appears to be completely uncharacteristic of Jesus. Early in the morning He is on His way from Bethany to Jerusalem and feeling hungry goes to pick some figs. Finding none He curses the tree with the words, *'May no one ever eat fruit from you again.'* What prompted such an action seeing that Mark tells us *'it was not the season for figs'* (v. 13)?

Each year the fig tree yields two, and sometimes three crops of fruit causing it to bear figs for up to ten months in the year. The late figs produce the main crop in August through to winter and the winter (or green) figs appear towards the end of March and ripen by mid-year.

As the incident occurred just prior to Passover it was probably early April and the green figs would have been at the start of their growth and not ready for picking for another two months.

The picture becomes clearer when we realise that the fruit of the fig appears at the same time as the leaves and often before them. Although not the season for figs the tree was in leaf and so it was reasonable to expect there would be fruit also.

Perhaps this tree which is naturally slow-growing had benefited from a secluded spot that had served as a sun-trap which accelerated its growth; the leaves were there – the fruit was not! In a sense the tree was proclaiming a false message, a promise it was not fulfilling. The leaves were really saying, 'Here is fruit!' but it was a lie! The tree was barren.

It seems Jesus saw in the tree a living visual aid. It was living a lie, its leaves were hypocritical and that summed up much of the nation's leadership. He had said as much during the years of His ministry and it came home with great force in His cleansing of the Temple.

Those leaders proclaimed a message but were devoid of the fruit it should have produced. They said one thing but did another. The Temple precincts had been full of bustling activity, religious exercises, but no evidence of fruit to glorify God. Cheating, lying, hypocrisy had effectively prevented any fruit from growing!

We must not fall into the same trap; we must never become all leaves and no fruit!

The Almond Encourages us to be Watchful

Growing up to 25 feet in height the almond is the first tree to flower in the year bearing pink and white clusters of blossom that appear before the leaves; besides being popular for eating, the nuts can be used in the production of oil and ointments.

A well-known Bible reference to the almond concerns the budding of Aaron's rod that produced fruit overnight (Numbers 17:8). Just as exciting is God's play on words in underlining a great truth when speaking with Jeremiah in chapter 1:11, 12:

> *The word of the Lord came to me,*
> *'What do you see, Jeremiah?'*
> *'I see the branch of an almond tree,' I replied.*

> *The Lord said to me,*
> *'You have seen correctly, for I am watching to see that my*
> *   word is fulfilled.'*

The Hebrew words for 'almond' (*'shoqed'*) and 'watch-fulness' (*'shaqed'*) only differ by one letter and it is as if God, by a play on words is telling Jeremiah that the almond – *shoqed* – is to remind him of God's faithfulness in watching – *shaqad* – over His word to see that it accomplishes all that He intends for it.

At the beginning of 1988, a few weeks after the start of the 'intifada' (the Palestinian uprising – literally, the 'shaking off') Jerusalem experienced an abundance of almond blossom greater than anyone could ever remember. Some Bible students accepted it as God's encouragement to His people that despite the start of a very difficult time He was still watching over events in order to bring to pass all that He had promised in His Word.

God's promises are for all time, as certain now as they ever were – take hold of them, embrace them and let them take root in your heart and mind.

The Grapevine Illustrates Abundance and Fruitfulness

Grapes and figs were often grown together with the vine being supported by the fig tree. Grapes formed an important part of the ancient Hebrew diet, some of the harvest being stored in the form of raisin cakes as well as the obvious production of wine.

From many Old Testament references to the grapevine, the incident speaking of abundance concerns the spies returning from searching out the Promised Land (Numbers 13). They penetrate north of Hebron to the valley of Eschol (lit. 'cluster') and, in addition to pomegranates and figs find such huge branches of grapes that it takes two men to carry one back to camp!

The observant tourist will notice that this incident is the emblem adopted by the Israeli Tourist Board.

The Lord's teaching of the Vine and Branches is included under the Eim Kerem entry.

The Pomegranate – Sweetness and Good Deeds

The pomegranate tree has many branches bearing dark green leaves and bright red flowers. The apple-shaped fruit has thick jackets containing hundreds of red, juicy seeds that make a refreshing drink. The flowers have medicinal properties whilst the bark and rind, once used in the production of ink is used for tanning purposes.

It has been associated with fertility because of its many seeds whilst some Jewish scholars say the perfect pomegranate contains 613 seeds identifying it with the number of commandments they are required to keep.

The fruit has featured widely in Jewish art embellishing the two great bronze pillars of the Temple (1 Kings 7:18) as well as being embroidered on the hem of the High Priest's robe. We are told that the shape of the fruit inspired the design of the crowns that adorn the Torah scrolls. They are called *'rimmonim'* which is Hebrew for 'pomegranates'.

The Mustard Tree – Growth and Faith

Some scholars have argued that the Kingdom of God and the Kingdom of Heaven are two separate entities. Without going into their reasonings it is interesting to note that when Jesus uses the grain of mustard seed to illustrate the growth of the Kingdom, Matthew refers to the parable as the 'Kingdom of Heaven' (Matthew 13:31) whilst Mark prefers the term 'Kingdom of God' (Mark 4:30)!

What an exciting visual aid to depict growth! The mustard plant really does become a tree, albeit a spindly one that can reach 10 feet or more in height and certainly support many birds – and the seed from which it grows is just like a pencil dot!

Perhaps even more telling is when Jesus says we only need to have faith like a mustard seed – a pencil dot – to move mountains! That sounds fantastic but as we progressively accept all that He teaches and put it into practice we shall continually be amazed at the power and love of our God!

'Have faith in God', Jesus answered.
'I tell you the truth, if anyone says to this mountain, "Go throw yourself in the sea," and does not doubt in his heart

*but believes that what he says **will happen**, it will be done for him.*

*Therefore I tell you, whatever you ask for in prayer, **believe that you have received it, and it will be yours**.*

And when you stand praying, if you hold anything against anyone, forgive him, so that your Father in heaven may forgive you your sins.' (Mark 11:22–26)

PART IV

The Feasts of the Lord
and how they speak of Jesus and God's plan of salvation

Also some other Jewish Festivals

The Jewish Calendar

Nissan	(March–April)
Ivyar	(April–May)
Sivan	(May–June)
Tammuz	(June–July)
Av	(July–August)
Elul	(August–September)
Tishri	(September–October)
Cheshvan	(October–November)
Kislev	(November–December)
Tevet	(December–January)
Shevat	(January–February)
Adar	(February–March)

The Jewish (lunar) calendar has 354 days as against the solar calendar of 365; unless adjustments are made to harmonize the two, the cumulative effect of 11 days discrepancy each year would cause the timing of the various Feasts to violate what is laid down in the Bible. The two are reconciled by adding an extra month (*Adar* 2) every two or three years – actually seven times in a 19-year cycle.

In addition, each year a day is added to or subtracted from the 'swing' months *Cheshvan* and *Kislev* according to whatever adjustment is needed.

The ancient rabbis believed that God created the world in the first week of *Tishri* (7th month) and so 1st of *Tishri* marks the beginning of the Jewish New Year – *Rosh Hashanah*. Years are reckoned from their dating of the creation, thus 1998 is the Jewish year 5758/9.

In Exodus 12 God had said that the first month of the year was to be *Abib*, a Canaanite word meaning 'ear' (at this time the barley grain was in the ear) but later it was changed to the Babylonian name Nissan.

Exodus 23 records that all the Jewish males had to appear before the Lord three times a year, each occasion being a time of harvest; thus they would have a perpetual reminder of the wonder of their deliverance from slavery as well as their dependence upon God for continued blessing in the Land to which He had brought them.

The Feasts of the Lord

Leviticus 23 is a useful framework for looking at the main Feasts and we commence with verse 5.

Pesach (Passover – Leviticus 23:5)

This is celebrated on 14th *Nissan* and is the first of the three 'pilgrim festivals'. It commemorates the great deliverance of the Israelites from Egypt (Exodus 12) and sees the commencement of the seven-day Feast of Unleavened Bread and the bringing to the Lord of the Firstfruits of the barley harvest.

The spiritual truth pictured in the Passover is quite clear. Just as those who were trusting in the shed blood of the lamb to protect them were secure in God's promise (*'when I see the blood I will pass over you'* (Exodus 12:13) – from a Hebrew verb 'to protect and defend'), so all who trust in the shed blood of God's Lamb Jesus, are secure from God's wrath against sin, which is eternal separation from Him.

A detailed account of the relationship between the Passover, Seder and the Lord's Supper follows later.

The Feast of Unleavened Bread

Commencing at Passover this was a seven-day reminder of God's faithfulness and salvation, the haste of their departure from Egypt and the need to be obedient and keep themselves free from sin.

The Sheaf of Firstfruits (Leviticus 23:10, 11)

This has an exciting truth pictured in it that becomes apparent in connection with that last Passover Jesus attended.

Remembering that Jewish days are reckoned from sunset to sunset, the Passover lamb was killed on the 14th *Nissan* (sometime between Thursday night and Friday night) and the 15th was the Sabbath (Friday night to Saturday night). The Sheaf of the Firstfruits of the harvest, which at this time would have been barley, was to be waved before the Lord 'on the day after the Sabbath' (v. 11). That day (16th *Nissan*) was Sunday – and that Sunday was Resurrection Day!

For years the presenting to God of the firstfruits of the barley harvest had been like a prophetic finger pointing to a future wonderful miracle that became fulfilled in Jesus! On that Resurrection Morning as the sheaf was being waved the 'firstfruits' of whom it spoke had been raised and became alive forever more!

When speaking about the resurrection, no wonder the apostle Paul says in 1 Corinthians 15:20 that *'Christ has indeed been raised from the dead, the firstfruits of those who have fallen asleep'*!

Shavuot – Feast of Weeks (Leviticus 23:5 – Pentecost)

This is the second 'pilgrim festival' coinciding with the wheat harvest and is celebrated on 6th *Sivan*. It is also known as the Day of Firstfruits as it marked the beginning of the fruit harvest.

From the day when the Sheaf (which weighed an omer – probably about two quarts) was waved before the Lord, 50 days were counted; known as Counting the Omer, it culminated with a new grain offering being offered to the Lord. As Greek influence increased the 50th day became known as Pentecost.

This offering was two loaves baked with fine wheat flour – and **leaven**. Apart from the peace offerings for thanksgiving this was the only cereal offering during the year that was baked with leaven. In the Bible leaven is nearly always symbolic of sin. The Passover bread was **unleavened** symbolizing the purity of the lamb and prophetically of Jesus; the two Shavuot loaves were **leavened** underlining the sin of the people. But why two loaves?

Perhaps they were prophetic, one representing Israel and the other the Gentile nations? Throughout the centuries, year after year, the loaves had made a dramatic declaration that the two peoples could be one before the Lord. Fifty days after the resurrection of Jesus 'when *Shavuot* (Pentecost) was fully come' (Acts 2:1) the Holy Spirit descended and the picture became a reality. The redemption established at Calvary was sealed at Pentecost and all nations both Jew and non-Jew could be one in the long-promised Messiah!

In the courtyard of the Temple, a wall some $4\frac{1}{2}$ feet high divided the Court of the Gentiles where everyone could walk, from the remainder of the complex reserved for Jewish people. Gentiles were forbidden to pass through the openings in this wall; notices warned that those trespassing only had themselves to blame for their ensuing death!

In the second chapter of Ephesians, Paul seems to be referring to this barrier when he says **the middle wall of partition** – the dividing wall – has been removed and Jew and Gentile have now become God's new person. The Gentile doesn't have to become a Jew and the Jew doesn't have to give up their Jewishness – all are one in Jesus the Messiah!

Centuries ago the rabbis calculated that *Shavuot* coincided with the giving of the Law at Mt Sinai and so the 19th and 20th chapters of Exodus are read in the synagogues. In addition, the love-story of Ruth and Boaz which is played out against the harvest fields around Bethlehem is also read. For believers, this is a lovely prophetic picture of the work of Jesus.

In Deuteronomy 25 we are told that when a married man died leaving no children, his brother or near relative had to marry the widow in order to raise children to perpetuate the dead man's name.

The widow had the responsibility of taking the initiative and in the story Ruth goes to Boaz who is not, in fact the nearest relative. He does the correct thing – he goes to the city gate and when that nearest relative comes along he speaks with him having requested ten of the city elders to be witnesses. He asks if the man is willing to redeem a plot of land belonging to Naomi, Ruth's mother-in-law, but in so doing must marry Ruth as part of the redemption.

Usually the widow would have approached the relative at the city gate and if he was unwilling to perform his duty she would remove his sandal and spit in his face as a sign of her outrage, and his family would then be known as 'the family of the unsandaled one'.

However, Ruth leaves the transaction to Boaz. The relative, maintaining his inability to fulfil that which was required of him removes his own sandal signifying he relinquishes all rights to walking on the land in question – and any claim upon Ruth – allowing Boaz to take his place. This is known as becoming the *'goel'*, the kinsman-redeemer.

Boaz, the Jewish kinsman-redeemer performs his duty towards Ruth who, being a Gentile had previously declared her trust in the God of Abraham, Isaac and Jacob (Ruth 1:16). Jew and Gentile become one in Father-God and their first child Obed is destined to become the grandfather of David and the ancestor of Jesus Himself, the greatest Redeemer!

'To redeem' is literally 'to buy back on paying the price' and just as Boaz redeemed Ruth who became his very own and a vital part of God's family, so Jesus redeems those who will dare to believe in Him, and they become permanently His, bought back out of Satan's kingdom of darkness and adopted forever into the family of God!

The Feast of Trumpets

Leviticus 23:24 says that 1st of *Tishri* was to be a rest, a reminder by the blowing of trumpets and a holy assembly. The verse doesn't explain what the people need to be reminded of but the rabbis teach that it is to bring to remembrance the people's covenant relationship with their Lord and a call to repentance.

By tradition, the *shofar* is blown every day of the month preceding the Feast of Trumpets and then 100 times on the day itself. It is thought this would so confuse Satan, whom they believed would be making an all-out effort to accuse them before the Lord at the start of the days of repentance, that he would think Messiah had come and give up the struggle!

The trumpet (*shofar*) was usually made of ram's horn in honour of Abraham's obedience concerning his test to sacrifice Isaac, and God's provision of a substitute ram (Genesis 22).

Rosh Hashanah (Levitucus 23:24)

This means the Head of the Year and is the Jewish New Year, the day when the Feast of Trumpets is celebrated. It is not mentioned in Jewish writings before the Mishna was completed in the second Century AD and probably dates from when the Israelites returned from their Babylonian exile under Ezra/Nehemiah – ?450 BC.

Legend has it that on this day three Books are opened in heaven; in one are written the names of the Righteous – those who are promised a good year. The book of the Wicked lists those who are condemned to death during the year.

The third Book contains the rest of the names for whom judgement is deferred for 10 days known as the Days of Awe or Repentance, at the end of which their names will be entered in one of the other two Books!

Hence New Year cards are exchanged with the greeting 'May you be inscribed for a good year'; in other words 'at the end of the 10 days may your name be found in the Book of the Righteous!' Accompanying this greeting, visitors will often be offered apple dipped in honey with the wish for 'a good, sweet year'.

During the morning of *Rosh Hashanah* lengthy services will be held in the synagogues stressing repentance, forgiveness and a turning to God. During the afternoon Orthodox Jews observe the ceremony of *Taschlich* ('cast off' in Hebrew) which graphically brings to life a wonderful Old Testament promise recorded in Micah 7:19; '(God will) *hurl* (cast) *all our iniquities into the depths of the sea.'*

Going to some stretch of moving water and accompanied by penitential prayers, pockets are symbolically
emptied allowing crumbs to fall and be carried away, never
to be seen again! A wonderful picture illustrating how God
deals with the sin of all who are trusting in Jesus for
salvation and forgiveness.

'To forgive' literally means 'to send away from one's self,
to let go', a truth King David knew 1000 years before
Calvary, for in Psalm 103 he speaks of the Lord as the one
who *'forgives all my sins and heals all my diseases'* (verse 3)
and later says, *'as far as the east is from the west, so far has he
removed our transgressions from us'* (verse 12). An even more
telling picture is seen in the ceremony that was enacted in
the Temple on *Yom Kippur*.

Yom Kippur – the Day of Atonement (Leviticus 23:27–32)

'Yom' is 'day' and *'Kippur'* means 'covering' as well as
'atonement'. *Yom Kippur* completes the Days of Awe and
repentance when pious Jews will have endeavoured to put
right anything that may have caused upset, distress, or
heartache in their own or other people's lives.

On this day Leviticus 23:27 says the people were to
humble their souls, and Jewish tradition sees this as
observing a fast throughout the day – usually a 25-hour
period ensuring the day was fully covered. As *Yom Kippur*
approached, the saying 'may you be inscribed for a good
year' was changed to 'may you be sealed for a good year',
expressing the hope for that person's name to be recorded
in the Book of the Righteous.

Leviticus 16 records the events of the Day of Atonement
when the High Priest took two goats and sacrificed one for
the sins of the people; laying his hand on the head of the
other he symbolically transferred to it the people's sins.
Known as the scapegoat it was then led away into the
wilderness never to be seen again. How wonderful that
the Lord Jesus became God's Scapegoat at Calvary and has
dealt fully and completely with the sin of all who will dare to
put their faith and trust in Him! What a wonderful Saviour!

Succot – Feast of Tabernacles or Booths (Leviticus 23:34–44)

The last of the three 'pilgrim festivals' is also known as the Feast of Ingathering because by now many of the fruits of the land would have been harvested and so it is a time for rejoicing.

Coming five days after *Yom Kippur* the Jews build booths in which to live for seven days commemorating the time when their ancestors lived in tents in the wilderness. Built on rooftops, balconies or in gardens, these flimsy dwellings are constructed of olive, myrtle or other tree branches. The sky must be visible through the roof and during the week the family take their meals in them, sometimes sleeping there as well.

In the synagogues four species are carried in procession; they are the *'etrog'* (citron), *'lulav'* (palm branch), the *'hadas'* (myrtle) and the *'arava'* (willow). They are said to represent aspects of human life and character and are waved in various directions which in centuries past was said to ward off evil spirits.

In Temple times during the Feast there was a daily procession from the Temple to the nearby Pool of Siloam where a golden pitcher was filled with water; returning to the Temple it was poured out into a silver basin at the altar steps.

Although this was not a biblical injunction it symbolized the prayer for rain (so essential at this time when the growing season was starting and the early rains were due) and also an anticipation of the outpouring of the Holy Spirit.

John's gospel (7:37–39) records that on the last and greatest day of the Feast (when according to some authorities the water ceremony did not take place) Jesus stood and in a loud voice declared, *'If a man is thirsty, let him come to me and drink. Whoever believes in me, as the Scripture has said, streams of living water will flow from within him.'* Jesus constantly took real-life situations in order to promote spiritual truths.

Also, the day following the end of the Feast (during which time the Temple would have been ablaze with the light from huge golden menorah) Jesus was again in the Temple Courts. At one point He stated, *'I am the light of the world. Whoever follows me will never walk in darkness, but will have the light of life'* (John 8:12).

Whether people thought they were obeying the Law or just following the tradition of the Fathers, Jesus took the opportunity to declare His Messianic identity. How electrifying those statements must have sounded – they certainly produced opposition; I wonder how many came to believe?

Simchat Torah – 'Rejoicing over the Law'

This is celebrated two days after the end of *Succot* and brings to a close 23 special days of great significance. It is not a biblical observance as it didn't start until 2nd/3rd century AD.

During the year the entire five books of Moses are read in the synagogue and are completed on this day – and to ensure there is no gap in reading the *Torah* a fresh start is again made on the book of Genesis. It is a day of great rejoicing with singing, dancing and hand-clapping as the *Torah* is paraded and great attention paid to it.

If Jewish folk can get so excited about the words on paper, what immeasurable delight and satisfaction there will be when the paper leads them to the Person it proclaims!

Channukah – the Feast of Dedication

This is also called the Feast of Lights and it is celebrated on 25th *Kislev* for eight days. This is a non-biblical Feast and commemorates an outstanding event that occurred in 168 BC.

The Syrians (under Antiochus Epiphanes) had desecrated the Temple with idols and also by sacrificing a sow on the altar. Three years later the Jews, under Judas Maccabeus had regained control and wished to cleanse and re-dedicate the Temple. The *Talmud* tells us they were dismayed to find only enough Holy Oil to keep the seven-branched candlestick (*menorah*) lit for one day. However, the one day's supply miraculously burned for eight days until more could be prepared.

This is why the *Channukah* candlestick (called a *Channukiah*) doesn't have seven holders like the usual *menorah*. In fact, it has nine; eight holders for each of the traditional days and one holder called the servant (*shamash*) with which to light the others as it is forbidden for them to be lit from each other. The *Channukiah* is usually placed in a window so that it can be seen by those passing by, and the Feast is a time for fun and games, parties and the exchanging of gifts.

The Feast was being observed in the time of Jesus because John's gospel (10:22) tells of Him walking in Solomon's porch in the winter and says 'it was the Feast of Dedication'. At that time Jesus makes the great declaration that He gives eternal life to all who listen to His words, trust and follow Him – and no-one will ever snatch them from His hands!

Purim

Known as the Feast of Lots from a Persian word *'pur'* meaning 'lot' it is observed on 14th *Adar*. Again, this is not a Feast prescribed in the *Torah* as it commemorates an event that occurred after the *Torah* was completed.

It happened in the 5th Century BC and recorded in the book of Esther – the only book in the Bible where God is not mentioned. It is presumed that as the Scroll of Esther was sent out in letter form the name of God was omitted in case the letters were damaged and the divine name desecrated. However, it is full of His overruling, with justice and right prevailing over the evil intentions of Satan working through the man Haman.

He was the Persian king's prime minister and determined to kill all the Jews of the country and decided by *'pur'* (lot) when that date should be. Queen Esther, a Jewish girl, encouraged by her cousin Mordechai risked her own life by appearing before the king uninvited, to plead for her own people. She was successful and Haman was the one hung on the gallows he had intended for Mordechai.

Purim is truly a celebration and during the day when the Scroll of Esther is read in the synagogue, whenever Haman is mentioned he is booed, feet are stamped and all sorts of noisemakers are used as a way of 'erasing' his name!

Two other non-biblical Feasts are:

Tisha B'av

This is a fast day observed on 9th of *Av* commemorating the destruction of the First and Second Temples (586 BC and AD 70) believed to have occurred on the same date on each occasion.

Tu B'Shvat

Observed on 15th of *Shevat* this is the annual celebration of the New Year of Trees. They are planted in an atmosphere of fun and enjoyment.

Yom Haatzmaut

Israel Independence Day, celebrated on 5th *Iyar* as a public holiday commemorates Israel achieving Statehood on 14th May 1948, the first time for 2000 years. Special parades and festivities are the order of the day.

Yom Yerushalayim – Jerusalem Day

This is a public holiday on 28th *Iyar* and recalls the Israeli victory over the Arab armies during the Six-Day War of 1967 when the City was reunited under Jewish control for the first time since AD 70.

Passover (*Pesach*), *Seder* (order) and the Lord's Supper

It should come as no surprise that Judaism and Christianity are closely entwined. Isaiah tells us that the Lord chose the

Jewish nation to be witnesses to the fact that He alone saves and is the only true God (Isaiah 43:10–12); other verses record that the Jews were chosen to show forth His love and faithfulness (Deuteronomy 7:7, 8), to be a blessing to all people (Genesis 12:1–3), and a praise to Himself (Isaiah 43:21). All of those intents and purposes matured and became a reality in the Person of the supreme Jew – Jesus! To believing (Messianic) Jews He is *Y'shua Hamashiac*, Jesus the Messiah!

The events of the first Passover – the Great Escape from slavery – is both a wonderful miraculous fact as well as a graphic prophetic picture of the salvation that would be accomplished centuries later by God's perfect Lamb, Jesus!

The account of the Passover in Exodus 12:1–20 directed the Israelites to take a lamb – or a kid from the goats – on the 10th day of the first month (*Nissan*) and keep it until the 14th day, to ensure it was unblemished, when it was to be killed at twilight. Using bunches of hyssop, a member of the mint family with its stiff branches and hairy leaves, they were to apply the animal's blood to the lintel and the sideposts of the house in which they were sheltering. And God said, *'the blood will be a sign for you on the houses where you are; and when I see the blood, I will pass over you'* (verse 13).

The lamb was to be roasted, fire speaking of judgement; the bread to be unleavened (discussed earlier) and eaten with bitter herbs that spoke of the bitterness of their enslavement. The meal was to be eaten fully clothed, feet shod, staff in hand, ready for a hasty departure. From now on, at this time of the year, they were to observe a Feast as a memorial of God's great redemptive act. After 430 years in Egypt the Israelites were on their way to the Promised Land!

During biblical times whilst the Temple was standing, Passover was celebrated in Jerusalem. Each household or group of ten people, but not exceeding twenty would take a lamb to the Temple for sacrificial slaughter; the Priests removed the fat and burned it, the blood being collected and poured out at the altar.

The family then returned home for the roasting and eating. In the years following the destruction of the Temple and its sacrificial altar the Rabbis authorized the keeping of the Feast in local homes with a shankbone of lamb to replace the sacrificial animal.

The Bible enjoins every home to be completely free of leaven (Hebrew *'chametz'*) before Passover can be celebrated (e.g. Exodus 13:7) and so for some time beforehand the house undergoes a thorough spring-cleaning. Special pots and pans are reserved for Passover, or a thorough cleansing of the everyday utensils is carried out until everything is 'hospital clean'. Needful repairs and decoration will often be carried out at this time.

In addition it is necessary for all food containing leaven to be eaten or given away. However, because this could cause hardship where a quantity of food is concerned a system has been devised whereby, for a monetary consideration, goods can be 'sold' to a non-Jewish person who takes possession of them just for the Passover period; afterwards everything reverts to the original owner.

The house having been thoroughly cleaned, the husband carries out a symbolic search on the evening prior to Passover. Accompanied by any children present, he goes from room to room by candlelight armed with a feather and a wooden spoon. To add to the children's excitement of the occasion the mother will have placed in different rooms some bread crumbs which are gathered up into the spoon with the feather, all being wrapped together and burned the following morning.

We don't really know what the 'Jesus meal' consisted of but we can get some idea from today's observance.

The table is set with two candles and a large, blue-enamelled brass (*seder*) dish which is the focal point of the table. It has six circular indentations on which are displayed the following symbolic foods:

- *'zeroa'* – Hebrew for 'shankbone'. It is a reminder of the Passover lamb and God's outstretched arm of protection. Some families substitute the roasted neck of a chicken for the shankbone.
- *'baytza'* – a roasted hard-boiled egg that was a reminder of the regular sacrifices made in Temple days; some say it reflects mourning for the loss of the two Temples, one in 586 BC destroyed by the Babylonians and the other in AD 70 by the Romans.
- *'karpas'* – green salad vegetable such as lettuce or parsley that represents life created and sustained by Almighty God. It would be dipped into salt water as a reminder that life for the Israelites in Egypt was one of pain, suffering and tears.
- *'maror'* – bitter herbs, often horseradish, sliced or grated symbolising bitterness and sorrow, which is dipped in the *charoseth*. In addition, some authorities say other 'bitter herbs' are to be used such as watercress and radish.
- *'charoseth'* – a paste consisting of apples, nuts, dates, spices and wine picturing the clay from which the Israelites made bricks, plus sticks of cinnamon (or ginger) for the straw.

In addition there is salt water ('tears of bitterness') and *'matzah'* (unleavened bread) consisting of three cracker-like wafers in the form of a sandwich. Messianic Jews say these typify the sweet, sinless life of the Messiah with the striped appearance of the *matzah* and the holes being a poignant reminder of His flogging and crucifixion.

Four cups of wine, which is sometimes mixed with warm water are a most telling reminder of the blood of the sacrifice.

A Messianic *Seder* Meal

It follows a set Order of Procedure known as the *Seder*, which is aided by a narrative called the *Haggadah* – 'the telling or the showing forth'.

The whole meal is meaningful and full of emotion as those taking part identify with the history of the occasion as well as seeing the promises of a coming Messiah and all the blessings He will bestow fulfilled in Jesus!

What must the meal hosted by Jesus have been like? To think that the long-promised Messiah was actually presiding at the meal that was commemorating a mighty deliverance, which in itself was but a shadow of an even mightier deliverance He was soon to accomplish!

The Israelites in Egypt sheltered under the blood of the lamb to receive protection from the angel of death; soon the Lamb of God would offer His blood on a cross of wood to provide eternal protection from the consequence of sin for all who would dare to trust in Him!

The father of the family or the man who is presiding as host says 'As we kindle the festival lights we pray for the illumination of the Spirit of God to bring great meaning to our Passover celebration.'

Mother, or some other lady, lights the candles and prays 'Blessed are you, O Lord our God, ruler of the universe, who has set us apart by His Word and in whose name we light the festival lights.'

Each cup of wine is accompanied by a phrase from Exodus 6:6–8 and after a prayer of thanksgiving (*Kiddush*) the Cup of Sanctification is drunk with the first phrase 'I will bring you out from under the yoke of the Egyptians.' This is the cup taken by Jesus that is mentioned in Luke 22:17, 18.

The host, and sometimes all present, now ceremonially wash their hands.

> *Who may ascend the hill of the Lord?*
> *Who may stand in His holy place?*
> *He who has clean hands and a pure heart...*
>
> (Psalm 24:3, 4)

Was this the time when Jesus acted in the place of a servant and washed the disciples' feet in order to teach them the great lesson of true servanthood (John 13:3–17)?

Taking a sprig of parsley, symbolic of the hyssop used to apply the lamb's blood, it is dipped in salt water and eaten – a reminder that life is often immersed in suffering and tears.

In Exodus 12:26 God says, *'when your children ask you, "What does this ceremony mean to you?" then tell them . . .'* – and a young member of the family always has the privilege of asking, 'Why is this night different from all other nights?'

He wants to know why they are only eating *matzah* instead of a choice between bread or *matzah*; why only bitter herbs instead of other vegetables; why they dip them twice whilst normally not even once and why they are eating reclining to the left rather than the choice of sitting or reclining.

This affords the leader of the meal a wonderful opportunity to paint in the Scriptural background to the meal whilst adding relevant teaching for daily living.

So, in addition to explaining the reason for only eating *matzah* (Exodus 12:8, 15) he might point out that leaven is often a reminder of sin and the need to break with sinful habits and start a fresh, new life (1 Corinthians 5:6–8). Furthermore, he could bring new meaning to the three *matzot* (the plural form of *matzah*).

Wrapped together in a napkin, these three wafers were known as a Unity. According to some rabbis it was the unity of the patriarchs Abraham, Isaac and Jacob, whilst to others it spoke of worship – the priests, Levites and the Israelite people.

But to believing Jews it was surely the Trinity of Father, Son and Holy Spirit! As we have said earlier the stripes on the *matzah* were an insistent reminder of Messiah being scourged (Isaiah 53:5) and the holes of His being pierced (Zechariah 12:10).

The middle wafer is removed, broken in half and one piece wrapped in a napkin just as Messiah was broken and wrapped for burial. It is known by the Greek word *'afikomen'* (meaning 'dessert') which is given various

Hebrew meanings including 'He came'! Instructing the children present to cover their eyes it is hidden until later in the evening when the children search for it; the host 'redeems' it from the finder for a suitable ransom gift!

The other half is now shared and an explanation given concerning the bitter herbs, after which some horseradish is scooped onto a piece of *matzah* producing 'tears of compassion' for their ancestors' sorrow. The *matzah* is dipped a second time in the horseradish but then into the sweet *charoseth* before eating it which reminds those present that even the most bitter of circumstances can be sweetened by the Presence of God in their lives.

At this point the host might recall the account of the impending betrayal of Jesus by one of those eating at the table with Him (Mark 14:17–21).

There is a custom in the Middle East concerning the Passover meal in which the head of the family takes a piece of *matzah* and after dipping it in the bowl places it in his wife's mouth as a token of his very deep love for her. Was Jesus telling Judas by a similar action that His love for this man remained steady and strong despite the awful thing he was about to do?

The answers to the four questions conclude with the explanation that slaves had to stand in the presence of others, or sometimes sit, but free people could recline when they ate and at Passover they wanted to emphasise their freedom by reclining.

The background story of the Passover is now given and when the account of the plagues is reached the second cup of wine is poured. This is the Cup of Plagues and as each plague is mentioned everyone repeats it three times, each time dipping the little finger into the cup and allowing a drop of wine to fall onto a napkin, thus reducing the cup's contents. This is to underline the truth that a full cup is a symbol of joy but that joy is reduced as the great cost of redemption is remembered.

The cup is retained as the host lifts the shankbone and retells the sacrifice of that first Passover lamb and the protection its blood gave to those who were obedient. Obviously, the opportunity is not lost to show how perfectly Jesus became the sacrificial lamb and that believers are redeemed by His precious blood (1 Peter 1:18, 19).

The roasted egg is mentioned. It signified the Temple sacrifices, as well as being a symbol of mourning – and by some as denoting new birth and eternal life.

The Cup of Plagues is now drunk with the second phrase from Exodus 6:6 *'I will free you from being slaves.'* After giving thanks supper is served although since the destruction of the Temple in AD 70 it has not included lamb.

When supper is over the children search for the *afikomen* which is redeemed by the host and shared as a dessert, the final food of the Passover.

Luke 22:20 records that after supper Jesus took the cup; this would have been the third cup which Paul calls the cup of blessing when writing to the believers at Corinth (1 Corinthians 10:16) but more usually known as the Cup of Redemption. It is drunk with the third phrase 'I will redeem you with an outstretched arm and with mighty acts of judgement'.

How wonderful and amazing that the promised Messiah Himself was actually offering the disciples a cup that spoke of the New Covenant that God was going to establish in the shedding of His Lamb's blood not many hours hence!

A later addition to the Passover is the cup of Elijah. Many Jews believe he will herald the Messianic age and the time of redemption. The cup is filled and the door of the house opened to show how welcome the Prophet will be; an act indicative of Jewish faith over the years that the Messianic age will come bringing a return to the Land and a time of freedom, harmony and peace, a time when the Lord shall be King over all the earth.

Some confirm this truth with words from Exodus 6:8:

> *And I will bring you to the Land which I swore to give to Abraham, Isaac and Jacob, and I will give it to you for a possession; I am the Lord.*

Whilst those trusting in Jesus can rejoice now in the forgiveness of sin and the gift of Eternal Life, they echo this longing for the time when Jesus will return to establish His Kingdom and to be seen indeed as the King of all kings and the Lord of all lords!

The *Seder* ends with drinking the Cup of Praise together with the fourth declaration 'I will take you as my own people and I will be your God' – and the traditional wish that Passover will be celebrated 'next year in Jerusalem'!

During the evening there would have been times of singing from the Hallel, Psalms 113–118. The gospel accounts of Matthew and Mark record that after supper and before leaving for the Mount of Olives the disciples sang a hymn; this would certainly have been a part or all of Psalm 118. Meditate on the wonder and emotion of Jesus singing words like these:

> *In my anguish I cried to the Lord*
> *and He answered by setting me free.*
> *The Lord is with me; I will not be afraid.*
> *What can man do to me?*   (Psalm 118:5–6)

> *I will not die but live,*
> *and will proclaim what the Lord has done.*
> *The Lord has chastened me severely*
> *but He has not given me over to death.*
>   (Psalm 118:17–18)

> *The stone the builders rejected*
> *has become the capstone;*
> *the Lord has done this*
> *and it is marvellous in our eyes.*
> *This is the day the Lord has made;*
> *let us rejoice and be glad in it.*   (Psalm 118:22–24)

Jesus was singing these words written a thousand years earlier that have such perfect and direct application to His situation; He builds Himself up with the very food of Scripture – God's Word!

He reminds Himself that in God there is ultimate freedom and nothing to fear; although rejected by the Leaders and the people under their control He sings prophetically that He is indeed the very Foundation Stone upon which the whole of God's Kingdom must be built. It can only be brought about by His taking the punishment for the sin of the world and then triumphing over it. He is determined to do His Father's will.

So as He prepares to leave the upper room for Gethsemane and all the horror, pain, suffering and excruciating torture leading to death, He sings,

> *This is the day the Lord has made;*
> *let us rejoice and be glad in it.'*

Isn't that absolutely fantastic!

Index

Index